PERSPECTIVES IN SOCIAL INQUIRY

CLASSICS, STAPLES AND PRECURSORS IN SOCIOLOGY

PERSPECTIVES IN SOCIAL INQUIRY
CLASSICS, STAPLES AND PRECURSORS IN SOCIOLOGY

Advisory Editors
ROBERT K. MERTON
ARON HALBERSTAM

FACTORS DETERMINING
HUMAN BEHAVIOR

ARNO PRESS
A New York Times Company
New York — 1974

Reprint Edition 1974 by Arno Press Inc.

PERSPECTIVES IN SOCIAL INQUIRY
ISBN for complete set: 0-405-05490-4
See last pages of this volume for titles.

Manufactured in the United States of America

————◆————

Library of Congress Cataloging in Publication Data

Harvard Tercentenary Conference of Arts and Sciences,
    Cambridge, Mass., 1936.
    Factors determining human behavior.

    (Perspectives in social inquiry)
    Reprint of the ed. published by Harvard University
Press, Cambridge, Mass., in series: Harvard ter-
centenary publications.
    1. Psychology—Congresses. 2. Human behavior—
Congresses. I. Title. II. Series: Perspectives in
social inquiry. III. Series: Harvard tercentenary
publications.
BF21.H3 1936a   150   73-14153 ✓
ISBN 0-405-05500-5

HARVARD TERCENTENARY PUBLICATIONS

FACTORS DETERMINING HUMAN BEHAVIOR

LONDON : HUMPHREY MILFORD

OXFORD UNIVERSITY PRESS

FACTORS DETERMINING
HUMAN BEHAVIOR

CAMBRIDGE, MASSACHUSETTS

HARVARD UNIVERSITY PRESS

1937

PREFACE

THE Harvard Tercentenary Conference was a part of the University's corporate expression of gratitude to all who have built and enriched her life. Harvard men have always been proud of the high courage which marked their Puritan forebears. They may be equally proud of the intellectual level of that little band. In 1643 the graduates of Cambridge and Oxford who had migrated to New England numbered 130, and constituted in the population a higher proportion of university-trained men than was again seen until the twentieth century. If we turn to the English counterpart, we find that the Royal Society germinated in Oxford during the period of Puritan domination and that the brother-in-law of Oliver Cromwell was a leader of that scientific movement. Another leader, and one of the strongest forces in what he called the "invisible college," was Robert Boyle, who has left on record significant and weighty statements of his ideals as a scholar and experimenter. He speaks of "that noble and improvable faculty which enables an Ingenious man to pry into the innermost Recesses of Mysterious Nature," and goes on to a memorable phrase, "that noble and improvable faculty whereby an Inquisitive Soul may expatiate itself through the whole Immensity of the Universe." Thereby Boyle takes his stand with his master Bacon, points clearly to the common basis of all our knowledge, and upholds its unity.

From these developments we may divine something of what must have been in the minds of the men who founded Harvard. They were concerned with learning as a whole, and the committee charged with the organization of the Tercentenary Conference was faced with the obligation of trying to do something which should in a measure correspond to their ideals. Accordingly, while providing to the best of their facilities for those aspects of knowledge which did not seem to admit of being grouped, they planned three symposia: Factors Determining Human Behavior; Authority and the Individual; Independence, Convergence, and Borrowing in Institutions, Thought, and Art. These symposia, unlike the rest of the Conference, called for the collaboration of scholars working in diverse fields of science and learning and thereby cut across conventional academic disciplines. Thus we had on one platform three groups of eminent men who contributed, each from the standpoint of his own special experience, with his own characteristic way of thought and his own method of study, to a common understanding of the vast problems of human behavior. The first symposium thus begins with our inner makeup and treats the forces which condition or impel human conduct; the second proceeds to the consideration of the economic, social, political, and intellectual factors in the structure of society which act upon the individual through social institutions and through accepted ideas; the third traces the yet broader interrelations and approximations observable in peoples separated by time or space.

In these days many delight in taunting the scholarly world with the charge of specialization and in repeating against our universities the old quip of "Knowing more and more about less and less." However, the men within academic walls know that the essential unity of the learned world is manifested by a common origin, a common history, and a common tradition preserved for nearly a thousand years in the universities. Scaliger, Casaubon, Grotius; Harvey, Descartes, Newton — they are our heroes just as they were the heroes of an earlier age. To use the words of a writer of the twelfth century, "We are like dwarfs, sitting on the shoulders of giants, in order that we may see things more numerous and more distant than they could see, not, certainly, by reason of the sharpness of our own vision or the tallness of our bodies, but because we are lifted and raised on high by the greatness of giants."

The great men of the past could survey all or a great part of the domain of knowledge as then understood. The expansion of that domain has of necessity entailed specialization: but only a superficial observer will hold that specialization leads mainly to sterility. Hitherto, in the whole history of our race, it has in fact had a beneficial influence upon the progress of general knowledge. Specialization gives rise to skill and to method. These in turn lead to the formation of a new department of knowledge. Then interactions are set up between this department and other departments, new or old, and thereby the cycle is completed and still another special field of study comes in view. Meanwhile, the interactions continue. With the multiplication of specialties they become more numerous, and general knowledge increases. The symposia reported in the present book and in the two companion volumes are presented as illustrations of such interaction: *sed nondum finis*.

CONTENTS

FACTORS DETERMINING HUMAN BEHAVIOR

THE NERVOUS SYSTEM

EDGAR DOUGLAS ADRIAN, M.D., D.Sc., LL.D.

*Foulerton Professor of the Royal Society (Physiology),
University of Cambridge*

THE lower creatures do not meet to discuss the factors which determine their behavior. "Know thyself" is a precept reserved for *homo sapiens*; indeed the more academic our discussion the better we shall demonstrate our true position in the animal kingdom.

We are animals with powers of reflection and foresight, who can use tools and form propositions. Our knowledge and attainments can increase from one generation to another because our children can learn from our successes and failures. In the last hundred years we have found out so much about the material world that we have acquired immense new powers of action on it. What have we found out meanwhile about ourselves?

There have been no practical achievements comparable to the radio set or the flying machine, but no one can doubt that ideas about human behavior are vastly different from what they were even fifty years ago. Our conduct is no longer as right or wrong as it was. We think of it still as the outcome of a conflict between opposing forces, but we do not postulate forces wholly good and wholly evil. In some lands they are now thought of as racial or class instincts: here we have more choice and are free, if we wish, to see ourselves driven by the more primitive forces which Freud has made respectable. But everywhere human behavior has become something to be studied by the methods of natural science, as objectively as possible.

As a foundation to this study there is a mass of information about the mechanism of the body. The behavior of any animal must depend in part on its general structure—its shape, size, number of limbs, arrangement of sense organs, etc., and with man there are the important structural modifications which allow the forelimbs to be used for wielding tools. Yet the chief factor which determines the range of our activities is the nervous system. Every movement is the result of the messages which pass from the central mass of nerve cells to the muscles, and the outgoing messages are varied according to the reports submitted by the sense organs. These show what is happening in the world outside, and the central nervous system must evolve a plan appropriate to the occasion. But only the simplest plans are possible if the central nervous system is ill-developed. The earthworm can take to its burrow when it feels the shock of footsteps on the grass, and such an immediate reaction needs only a few hundred nerve cells and fibers; but we can sell out an investment when we hear rumors that the company is unsound, and this reaction needs the ten thousand million cells of the human cerebral cortex.

Our concern is with behavior of this characteristically human type. It represents by far the most complex synthesis achieved by any nervous system. Neurology, therefore, is not to be blamed because it cannot yet analyze such a product into an affair of nerve networks and nerve impulses. But from one aspect human behavior is an affair of networks and impulses; it may be useful to picture it in these terms in spite of the fact that we know far more about our thoughts and actions than we do about the mechanisms in our brains.

The central nervous system may be divided into the forebrain, the cerebral hemispheres which elaborate the general plan of behavior, and the brain stem and spinal cord which have to carry out the plan and attend to the administrative details. The whole system is made up of cells with thread-like extensions, some running as nerve fibers to the periphery and some forming the interlacing networks of the central apparatus. The cells and their extensions are excitable; within them are stores of available potential energy, ready to be discharged as soon as the restraining forces are weakened but replenished as soon as the discharge is over. All nervous activity involves discharges of this kind. Thus the long distance signaling from sense organs to brain and from brain to muscles is carried out by the conduction down the nerve fibers of repeated impulses, momentary waves of activity traveling like the spark along a fuse. And everywhere in the nervous system energy is liberated in brief outbursts rather than in a continuous stream. This fact by itself has little bearing on our actions, save that it sets an upper limit to the rate at which activity can change. What is of more importance is the fact that in some nerve cells the outbursts seem to occur spontaneously, without the need for an external stimulus to start the discharge.

The best example is the respiratory center, the group of cells in the brain stem which controls the rhythmic movements of breathing. For these cells the normal state is one in which periods of rest and activity alternate regularly. There are various devices for controlling the rhythm and prolonging one or other phase to suit the convenience of the organism, but the regular cycle must return in the end, and it can occur, not from a sequence of reflexes, but from the cycle of breakdown and repair in the nerve cells. The movements of walking and running can be determined in the same way by an automatic rhythm in a group of nerve cells. With these, however, the organism has a greater measure of control and can start or stop the rhythm by the appropriate signals. The work of Coghill and others on the development of behavior in the embryo has shown that many complex activities have this same semi-automatic origin, the outside world giving signals to begin and end and the organization of the nerve cells determining the general plan of response.

Admittedly there can be no real separation of activities which are spontaneous from those which are evoked by the environment. It is of interest none the less to find that the region in which spontaneous activity seems most ready to occur is in the great surface network of the forebrain — the cerebral cortex. Even in deep anesthesia the cortex is alive with the electrical pulsations which are the index of nerve-cell activity. They vary from a simple rhythmic beat to an irregular succession of waves. The latter are not merely a reflection of the irregular world outside, for the anesthetic has cut off all incoming sensory messages; they are due rather to the automatic discharges of nerve cells, linked together, but differing in position and structure and in the past history of their activities. In these cells a steady state is impossible because their internal tension is constantly increasing to the point of discharge.

Although the cortex cannot be kept completely at rest for more than a few seconds, the degree of activity in it can vary enormously. The variations are due in part to the world outside and in part to the internal necessities of the nerve cells. Activity in one cell tends to foster activity in its neighbors and so to build up the general level of excitation. The level will rise until the process is checked by the falling reserves of available energy. Similarly, rest breeds rest, and this process is checked by the internal tensions rising ultimately to the point of breakdown. The sudden increase of activity when we wake in the morning illustrates the change of level brought about by external stimuli acting on a recharged nervous system, though other factors are concerned as well. Inhibition, the process by which one cell can suppress instead of enhancing the activity of other cells, is no doubt a factor which helps to shift the focus from one part of the cortex to another. In general, however, we may think of the forebrain as a complex society of nerve cells, the units of which cannot remain for long either in intense activity or in complete rest.

These electrical changes give a picture of cerebral activity which recalls certain features of mental activity. The environment can start or stop a train of thought and keep it within certain channels, yet the sequence of ideas is often dictated almost entirely by past events and certain sequences seem to obtrude themselves unbidden. Such comparisons are dangerous, for they suggest that we have already a reasonable knowledge of the connection between mental and neural events, whereas in fact we know almost nothing. We can be sure, nevertheless, that the connection is extremely close.

The activity of the cerebrum, determined largely by the past and continually changing even in a steady environment, is in sharp contrast with that of the rest of the central nervous system. This has no memory. Its function is to carry out the plans dictated by the cerebrum and at the same time to keep the machinery of the body running smoothly. It must regulate the intake of food and oxygen, the circulation of the blood, its temperature and acidity. It must keep the body in its correct position in space, balancing it in spite of its shifting center of gravity. It must minimize the disturbances which are likely to result from great exertion or injury. For all this there is a beautiful reflex machinery co-ordinating the messages from sense organs specially adapted to register the blood pressure, the tension in muscles, the pull of gravity, et cetera.

But an animal without its cerebrum is no more than an automaton: it can stand and breathe and live after a fashion, but its behavior is reduced to a number of reflexes or, at the most, habitual patterns of action.

Long ago Claude Bernard insisted that the internal environment must be constant if life is to be unrestricted. His dictum has been supported lately by two distinguished physiologists from the two Cambridges. Cannon has shown how the visceral nerves prepare the body for sudden emergencies and Barcroft has studied the factors which lead to a breakdown of normal activity. It is significant that man has more need of a constant environment than any other animal, since it is the cerebrum which has the most delicate organization and can least withstand any change.

Human behavior, then, is pre-eminently the affair of the cerebral cortex. This is made up of the same structures as the rest of the nervous system, though there are more nerve cells in it, larger networks in proportion to incoming and outgoing pathways, and more spontaneous discharge. What is new is its power to combine past activity with present. As Sherrington has said, "The great new surface net of the brain is educable. Before it, truly, there were educable systems in the animal world but this is so educable as to be practically a new thing in the world. In the dog it can acquire new links even in a few repetitions and links can be combined even to the third degree. In man it seems they can develop almost without limit."

The cortex can learn and can use its learning to generalize and to solve new problems. But even the simplest kind of learning involves a factor which must still be expressed in psychological terms. As Pavlov's work has shown, there must be interest, a prospect of reward or punishment, an emotional stress which will change to satisfaction when the lesson is learnt or the problem solved.

We are still quite ignorant of the neural changes which take place when new associations are formed in the brain, and we can only guess why an incentive is necessary. Twenty or even ten years hence we shall know much more, for there are definite changes in the electrical activity of different regions when we direct our attention from the visual field to the auditory and vice versa. These are not beyond analysis. It is perhaps too much to hope that in revealing the neural mechanism of attention they will reveal that of consciousness as well, but at least they may show what kind of influence is exerted by emotional interest and why that influence is exerted on particular mental and neural sequences.

We may guess that the state favorable to learning involves an increase of excitability and possibly a change in the chemical environment of those parts of the brain in which the new connections are established; and probably it is brought about by the more primitive parts of the forebrain, the hypothalamus and the basal ganglia. These regions prepare the nervous system for its cycle of sleep and waking; they are linked with the hormone system and they control various kinds of instinctive and emotional behavior. Sinister proof of their importance comes from cases of injury or disease. But whatever the regions concerned, it is safe to assume that there must be some activity on the emotional or instinctive level to direct the attention and prepare the brain for new associations.

For discriminative behavior, therefore, there must be some interest: yet if there is too much the behavior will cease to be discriminative. Under intense emotional stress the behavior tends to conform to one of several stereotyped patterns. These are managed by the more primitive parts of the forebrain, and the cortex has little to do with them beyond directing the behavior towards a particular

object. Bard has shown that a cat whose cortex has been destroyed may give all the signs of rage, though it is a blind rage
and useless to the animal. With the brain intact the rage is
directed. It is still a stereotyped response, but it is often the
best response for the cat to make, since its cortex has not
the capacity to plan more elaborately. In man, however,
the cortex, when it is allowed free play, can be far more
potent, and emotional reactions which force the behavior
along one line and allow no scope for discrimination are far
less so. Moreover, emotional reactions tend to spread
through all the members of a group and to build themselves
up to higher and higher levels.

There is no need to pursue a devious argument to its
certain but commonplace conclusion — that our behavior
will be most effective when there is enough emotional tension to arouse the activity of the forebrain but not enough
to submerge it in a stereotyped response. We know well
enough that our emotions can cloud our judgment, and
the psychologists have shown that they do so far more than
we suspect. We know that some interest is necessary,
that moral indignation supplies the driving force for great
reforms but that rage does not help them. Need we care
greatly whether the neurologist can produce a scheme of
nervous mechanism which will account for these things?

Most of us, I think, would welcome the knowledge
gained, but we might reasonably doubt whether it would
make us more effective units of society. It is, in fact, un-
likely that neurological research will give new methods of
control over human behavior. What it will certainly do
is to improve some of the methods which exist already —
for instance, the control of behavior by drugs. Tea and
alcohol are homely examples, and the new narcotics which
can give peace of mind before a surgical operation have
shown what we may expect in future from this method of

regulating our brains. For more continuous action there are the drugs which the body manufactures for itself — the hormones. These, fortunately, have a place reserved to themselves in today's discussion.

But when all is said a knowledge of physiology offers only one certain, though perhaps unattainable, method by which human behavior could be improved. That is to breed men with larger brains. Our cerebral hemispheres are not so much larger than those of the chimpanzee and contain no new structures, but our behavior is of a different order. We can pile one box on another without thinking: Professor Köhler's chimpanzees could succeed by chance, but the essentials of the problem were quite outside their mental range. It is tantalizing to think of the new relations we should see, of the new world of thought we should live in, if our brains were but twice their present size. Our behavior would then be superhuman: it would be determined by the same physiological factors, but the importance of the cortex would be so magnified that the result must be beyond the power of human thought.

HORMONES IN RELATION TO
HUMAN BEHAVIOR

JAMES BERTRAM COLLIP, PH.D., M.D., D.Sc., LL.D.

Professor of Biochemistry, McGill University

ALL who are familiar with the proved facts of endocrinology will, I think, unhesitatingly agree that the hormones, those chemical messengers produced by that specialized group of tissues known as the ductless glands or glands of internal secretion, play an essential role in the maintenance of normal bodily functions, both physical and mental, in the human individual. Hoskins[1] has said: "The evidence is now conclusive that what we are — physically, mentally, sexually and emotionally — depends in no small measure upon the functions of the endocrine glands. They cooperate in an important way in the regulation of our activities in health and modify the course when they do not primarily determine our diseases." I think that the significance of the internal secretions in relation to human behavior can be realized best if they are considered from the standpoint of their biological value. Any living animal organism, whether it be man — at the top of the evolutionary scale — or the jelly-fish — near the bottom — or any other of the various living things which are intermediary between these two, must be considered from the biochemical viewpoint as a machine. From time immemorial, from the dawn of life on the globe, environmental factors, together with the inherent properties of protoplasm, have contributed to a constant change in the types of living things. All of these have been more or less efficient machines, and of those types which have survived it may be said that they were adapted to their environment. There are two basic types of mechanism which are possessed by members of the animal kingdom, each of which plays a specific part in the regulation of the various functions and activities of the organism as a whole. These are the nervous system and the chain of endocrine glands. Professor Adrian has dealt already with the former. In the lower forms of animals, the great group Invertebrata, the nervous system is probably pre-eminent; in fact very little is known of the hormones or their functions in the invertebrates. The situation, however, in the vertebrate kingdom is quite different. Here, from fish to mammal without exception, we find the ductless glands represented in all forms and integrating with the nervous system in the control of the animal machine of which they form a part.

While there are vast differences between animals of different phyla and smaller but important differences between different species, there is as yet no reason to doubt, in so far as the hormones are concerned, that the active principle elaborated by a ductless gland in the fish does not differ materially from that elaborated by the same gland in man or other mammals. An excellent example of this is to be found in the case of insulin. An extract prepared from the principal islets of teleostean fishes or from the pancreas of the elasmobranch manifests the same physiological properties when tested upon a normal rabbit or a diabetic patient as does the insulin prepared from the pancreatic glands of cattle, pigs, or sheep. There may be quantitative differences relative to the effects of individual hormones of different animal origin, but qualitatively they give the same physiological effects in adequate test objects. But though the hormone may be the same from fish to man, its function in fish and man may conceivably be different. As Thomson[2] has pointed out in a discussion on the evolution of hormones, there are, on the one hand, cells which elaborate the specific chemical substance and, on the other, cells which respond to the presence of this substance once it is brought to them. There are examples of the apparently useless presence in relatively primitive organisms of chemical substances which in higher groups have acquired a physiological function as hormones. It may be, of course, that the significance of such substances as oestrin in insects, of adrenalin in annelids, of the oxytoxic posterior pituitary principle in fishes, is yet to be discovered, and that it may ultimately be established that all of these have a true hormone function in every form in which they are found. The point raised by Thomson of the lack of a complete parallelism in the phylogenetic development of hormones and in their functional manifestations is worthy of much further study.

A good example of the fact that the same hormone may act upon different types of tissue in different species is illustrated in the case of prolactin of Riddle. This anterior pituitary lobe principle stimulates the fully developed mammary gland of the guinea pig to milk secretion, and in the pigeon it causes the growth of a structure known as the crop gland, the development of which is essential for the production of crop milk. The underlying physiological effect is in each case the same, but the structures acted upon are very different. These two analogous organs must have developed separately their responsiveness to this anterior pituitary principle.

When an endocrine linkage is evolved, it probably represents a delegation of authority formerly resident elsewhere. As an example of this, sexual dimorphism of plumage in the sparrow is apparently controlled by the chromosomes of the individual epidermal cells, whereas in the fowl this control has been turned over to the presence or absence of the ovarian hormone. Again, testicular hormone is essential for the growth of antlers in the red deer but not in the closely related reindeer. These examples may serve to show that the delegated authority may easily be reassumed with but a small change in the genetic constitution. Failure to realize this has led to some of the wildest and least plausible speculations ever associated with any branch of science. It seems, for example, nothing short of fantastic to argue that because in white races destructive disease of the adrenal glands may tend to pigmentation of the skin, therefore the black races display under-development of this gland — forgetting that this should also condemn them to extreme muscular debility, infertility, et cetera. It seems, too, that similar pitfalls must await all those who argue that because many of the sufferers from some particular endocrine disorder have a characteristic gait or complexion or expression, all those who at first glance resemble them are necessarily sufferers from the same fundamental disorder.

Apart from exceptions of the type indicated above, it is the general rule that the function subserved by any particular hormone is much the same in all of the higher animals. I desire to emphasize this now especially because in any discussion as to the relationship of hormones to human behavior it is very easy to overlook basic principles, and in so doing to be led astray. Many such discussions in which due regard has not been had for fundamental ideas have unfortunately found their way into print. I fear that such writings are more apt to hinder than to accelerate progress in the application of the known facts of endocrinology towards the solution of such problems as are presented in this symposium today on factors relating to human behavior.

I should like now to direct my discussion from the animal kingdom in general to man in particular. It may be said of the individual man that his own peculiar character and physical make-up are the outcome of the phylogeny of his species and are the resultant of the special forces to which his progenitors have been subjected in the course of countless generations. While man as a living machine differs in no essential manner from the higher animals, he has a brain the frontal lobes of which have been developed to an extent not seen in other forms, even in the anthropoid apes. The evolution of modern man as a social being differing in so many respects from other species has of course been attributed to the specialized development which has taken place in this particular part of the brain. He is endowed not only with consciousness but with self-consciousness. Entirely apart from the basic importance of this latter to psychology, it is of great significance from the biological aspect. Man by virtue of his self-consciousness can think and in thinking can will, and in so doing he can modify in a most profound manner various bodily functions which are amenable to modification by nervous stimuli. In other words, the great development of the cerebral cortex in man has allowed of the opening up of new channels of nerve communications. The outgoing pathways from the central nervous system to the ductless glands are probably developed to much the same degree in the lower forms as they are in man; but in the latter, due to the further development of the brain, impulses can arise in higher centers which can motivate peripheral structures by way of the older pathways. As far as we know, practically all of the tissues and organs of the body are in direct connection with the central nervous system. The various ductless glands are no exception to this rule, and while much yet remains to be done in connection with the nervous control of these structures, it is safe to assume that all of the endocrine organs are directly or indirectly under nervous control. The extent to which, on the other hand, the nervous system itself is dependent upon or affected by individual endocrine gland secretions must be for the most part a matter of conjecture at this time. In connection with these two great systems, the nervous and the endocrine, we must recognize an integrative action not only in regard to their effects upon other structures but in their effects upon one another. So while it is true that man as a biological machine is similar to the animal, he has these two systems — the nervous and the endocrine — which may function on a higher level.

The behavior of the individual man is in part the expression of his conscious, self-conscious, and unconscious life. It becomes obvious, therefore, that the endocrine glands which, with the nervous system, have so much to do in the regulation of the various bodily functions, must in an indirect way influence profoundly his behavior.

Let us consider the hypothetical case of the normal man with normal behavior. The endocrine system of such an individual may be considered simply as a part (a very essential and important part) of this human machine. It functions continuously, now faster, now slower, in its various parts — all the while responding to stimuli both nervous and chemical, and liberating from its various components now more, now less of the individual internal secretions which play their role in the regulation of the various bodily functions. It may be said, because each of the various hormones contributes a definite part to the maintenance of the normal state of the body of this hypothetical individual, that each therefore has a definite effect upon his behavior. In dealing with a normal body and normal behavior, the relationship of hormones to the behavior pattern is not at once apparent, and the point of view just expressed might be thought by some to be unjustifiable. The evidence that certain types of abnormal behavior patterns are due to disturbances in the endocrine system is very convincing; also there are many examples of the behavior pattern being modified by too much or too little of some hormone. It would therefore seem logical to conclude that the normal behavior manifested by our hypothetical normal man is as much dependent upon hormones as certain alterations in the behavior pattern are dependent upon alterations in the hormone balance.

There are a variety of well established experimental as well as clinical results which demonstrate quite conclusively that the behavior of individuals may be altered owing to the presence of too little or too much of some hormone agent in the circulation. Such effects of hormones are usually indirect rather than direct. Some illustrations of this follow.

Thyroid disease is fairly common, and patients suffering from this type of disability may show evidences of overstimulation by the thyroid hormone or they may manifest the signs of thyroid hormone deficiency. All sorts and varieties of intermediate stages are of course met with clinically. The behavior patterns of the two types are diametrically opposed and each deviates far from normal. Barker has described these two types of thyroid disease as follows: The hyperthyroid type, as seen in the case of exophthalmic goiter, is hypersensitive to mental stimuli, is irritable and restless. Patients suffering from this malady often exhibit characteristic anomalies; sometimes they suffer from pathological fears, obsessions, or ideas of injury; occasionally they show marked excitement not unlike that seen in hypomanic states. In myxoedema, on the other hand, in which there is under-function of the thyroid gland, the patients present a strikingly different mental state and behavior. The facial expression is apathetic and quiet; the patients seem drowsy and dull; their thoughts come slowly and their emotional reactions are sluggish. Barker[3] emphasizes, however, that though there are profound changes in thinking, feeling, and striving in thyroid disease, it is relatively rare that outspoken psychoses occur either with frank over-function or under-function of the thyroid. When they do appear, he states, these psychoses appear to have their origin in an associated psychopathic inheritance rather than in endocrine anomalies alone.

One of the chief functions of the *parathyroid* glands is to regulate the level of calcium in the blood stream. The maintenance of normal tone in muscle and nerve is among other things dependent upon ionic concentration of calcium and other inorganic elements. A lowering of the calcium ion concentration disturbs this balance, and a hyperexcitable state of the nervous system is the main effect of such a change. There is a hyperexcitability of the entire nervous system in hypoparathyroidism, of which the resulting manifestation may be tetany. The opposite condition, a profound loss of muscle tonus, is occasionally met with in chronic cases. I recall one case in particular (which I saw some years ago) in which this condition of atonia was the predominant symptom. This patient was for a time considered to be a mental case. He could be roused from a stuporous state only with difficulty and his speech was incoherent. When it was found that his blood serum calcium was only half the normal value, appropriate treatment was instituted and his rapid return to normal both mentally and physically was truly remarkable.

Some of the most outstanding examples of the effects of

hormones on behavior are to be found in the field of sex physiology. Moreover, the remarkable researches that have been made of late by chemists working in this field have made available synthetic products which have the same physiological properties as the *male and female hormones* ordinarily found.

The general characteristics of "maleness" and "femaleness" are undoubtedly due to the action in the organism of the male hormone and the female hormone respectively. Also, there seems little doubt that the fluctuating concentration of sex hormones in the blood of woman is the basis for a number of altered behavior patterns so peculiar to the female. It may be confidently expected that great advances will be made in this subject in the near future, because accurate methods for the assay of certain of the hormones in the blood and secretions of the individual are being developed.

Although the *suprarenal glands* in man and the higher vertebrates appear on macroscopic examination to be a pair of discrete structures, actually they consist of two distinct types of tissue, one of which, the medulla, is developed in close association with the sympathetic nervous system; the other, the cortex, is more closely related to the genital organs in its development. Two definite and distinct hormones have been obtained from suprarenal tissue — adrenin and cortin — and there still remains the possibility that other active principles may be obtained from these very important endocrine glands. The symptoms which develop in patients with suprarenal gland disease depend upon which part is involved. Thus, there may be evidences of under- or over-activity of medulla or cortex or of both medulla and cortex. A discussion of the various types of suprarenal cases and their behavior characteristics would take us too far afield. Suffice it to say, since one suprarenal hormone (adrenin) is a sensitizer of the sympathetic nervous system, and abnormal functioning of the cortex may result in profound changes in the secondary characteristics of sex, that there is here a hormonal background for each of a variety of behavior patterns manifested by those suffering from suprarenal disease.

The hormone insulin produced by the islet tissues of the *pancreas* furnishes an excellent illustration of an indirect effect of an endocrine secretion upon behavior. In severe untreated cases of diabetes the blood sugar level is elevated and there is a condition of acidosis due to the presence in the blood stream of large amounts of the so-called acetone bodies. By the proper use of insulin the blood chemistry of these patients may be restored to normal and with this restoration of certain of the blood constituents to normal values there is as a rule a great change in the mental attitude and outlook. If, however, an overdose of insulin is given, or if adequate carbohydrate is not available, the blood sugar may fall below normal and, if this condition of hypoglycemia is allowed to progress, a convulsive seizure with loss of consciousness may result. During the time that the blood sugar is falling from the normal level to the convulsive level, various changes may occur in the patient's subjective sensations. There may be at first a sensation of hunger, to be quickly followed by faintness. The subject may gradually become inarticulate, although still quite conscious, but consciousness is soon lost and a convulsive seizure occurs. This, if untreated, may end fatally. A small quantity of sugar will in a few minutes restore a patient in hypoglycemic shock to normal.

The hormone adrenin raises the blood sugar by virtue of its ability to cause glycogen, which is present in the liver and muscles, to break down to glucose. Professor Walter Cannon and his colleagues[4] in their brilliant presentation have shown that the suprarenal glands may be activated in a number of ways to discharge adrenin; chief among these were pain, hunger, fear, and rage. A good example of this emergent function of the suprarenals was recently reported to me. I should like to quote it because it furnishes an excellent illustration of the effects of two hormones in the same subject.

A diabetic patient taking the insulin treatment realized one morning as he was walking down the street that he was developing an hypoglycemic reaction. Finding that he had forgotten to provide himself with a chocolate bar, he proceeded to the nearest drug store. By the time he reached the store his gait was unsteady and his speech incoherent. He tried to explain to the druggist what he wanted, but the latter, fully convinced that he was dealing with a drunken man, threw him into the street. The patient, still conscious and terribly enraged at being so treated, promptly recovered and proceeded to another store unaided, made his wants known, and continued on his way. Obviously we have here an example of the activation of the adrenals as a result of anger, leading to the release of enough adrenin to cause an increase in the patient's blood sugar sufficient to restore his equilibrium and his powers of speech.

Research work of the past few years in connection with anterior lobe physiology has established this organ as a master-gland among the endocrines. This is due to the fact that it exercises a trophic influence on a number of these, such as the thyroid, the suprarenal, and the gonads. Over-activity or under-activity of the *anterior pituitary* is therefore bound to result in changes in other glands. These will be over-stimulated or under-stimulated according as the anterior lobe is liberating more or less of the specific trophic principles. In cases of manifest disordered functioning of any of the pituitary-controlled ductless glands, the question always arises as to whether the particular gland in question is on an abnormal functional level due to a change in anterior lobe activity or whether the abnormal condition is due to a primary change in the gland or glands involved.

Because of this close functional association between the anterior pituitary and other glands of internal secretion, it is possible that most of a group of widely divergent cases of obvious endocrine disease may have one thing in common — namely, a primary functional disturbance in the anterior lobe. Clinicians will agree, I think, that most frank endocrine cases have abnormal behavior patterns, and since the dominance of the anterior lobe in the endocrine chain is established, it would appear that this gland and its various hormone products have more to do with behavior in the human subject than any other gland or glandular secretion.

While the variety of cases possessing altered anterior lobe function is great, two types are often referred to, to illustrate on the one hand the results of over-activity and on the other under-activity of this gland. The former is acromegaly and the latter pituitary dwarfism. In the early stages of acromegaly there may be obvious signs of hypergonadism and hyperthyroidism. Barker[3] states that marked mental disturbances, frequently of a hypomanic character, may be associated with this form of hyper-pituitarism. Most of these cases tend to show signs of failing pituitary function in later years, often accompanied by corresponding changes in mentality. Atkinson, writing on acromegaly, cites fifty-four authors who in their publications on this disease mention personality changes of varying severity from simple melancholia to manic depressive insanity and schizophrenia. As early as 1897, Brunet

stated that one-quarter of all cases on record within ten
years of the first case described by Pierre-Marie showed
personality changes. Cushing[5] found that in one form or
another psychic irregularities were manifested in the larger
number of patients suffering from this endocrine disease.

As a result of a critical investigation of many endocrine
cases, the late Allan Winter Rowe[6] concluded that frank
psychoses and less well defined psychoneuroses find a
definite representation in all of the groups of endocrine
disorder. He found that the prepubertal pituitary case
was frequently a child with a behavior problem. He found
that cases of pituitary disease manifesting the Fröhlich
syndrome usually had a genuine lowered mental acuity.
The adult pituitary cases studied by Rowe showed a definitely high percentage of individuals mentally normal.
Those who tended toward hyperfunction frequently
showed high intellectual capacity.

The pituitary dwarf is as a rule, in the early years at
least, within normal limits in so far as behavior is concerned. As the subject grows older, however, there may
develop an abnormal behavior pattern as an indirect result
of the hypopituitarism. The short stature and the hypo-
gonadism are the usual causes of the changed mental outlook which some of the older cases present.

A good example of marked behavior change in the dog,
which can be attributed to hormone treatment, is afforded
by the young animal that has been hypophysectomized
and then after several weeks is treated with a potent
hypophyseal extract. Cushing,[5] in his pioneer work on the
pituitary gland, described many examples of behavior and
personality changes which he had observed in his hypophysectomized dogs. The case of a wolf-hound puppy
studied recently in my own laboratory is of particular
interest in this connection. It was observed, soon after the

removal of the pituitary gland, that the animal, although belonging to a naturally aggressive stock, became extremely stupid and timid in his behavior. There was, in fact, a clear-cut deterioration in his behavior from the normal pattern of the wolf-hound puppy. After many months the animal was treated daily with an anterior pituitary extract. Within a few days the animal's general behavior and personality were markedly altered, so that he acted much more like the normal type. The change was so apparent that a worker in the laboratory, unaware that treatment had been started, commented upon the unusual activity of the animal and asked if anything had been done which might account for it.

Cases such as this, proving as they do that the level of intelligence in an animal can be raised as a result of the action of certain hormones, afford a background which should allow us to look forward with a greater degree of confidence to the possibility of applying the results of endocrine research to the solution of some of the problems of human behavior.

In the discussion thus far I have attempted to show that the endocrine system and its products the hormones constitute an essential part of the animal machine; since individual human behavior must of necessity be dependent upon the nature of the body which the subject possesses, it follows that hormones, one of the variable quantities in that body, can contribute both directly and indirectly to the particular pattern manifested at any one time. Let us now examine a little more closely into the mechanism by which hormones can influence human behavior. As a starting point, I cannot do better than to recall to you some of the principles of genetics which are applicable here. Since the development of each individual follows from the original union of two cells, the sex elements egg and sperm, it follows — whatever the outcome may be — that it has been predetermined in large measure by the character of these two cells. The fact that this predetermination is due to the chromosomes of the parent cells and the countless genes which they contain has long since been established by the research work of the geneticists. Some of the properties of the genes, the agents directly responsible for the transmission of hereditary characters, are worthy of note here, because of the important bearing which they have on the subject under discussion. They are able to reproduce themselves exactly; they are in a way independent of one another and each gene may have a separate or independent effect upon development; one gene may produce effects in more than one organ and many different genes may affect a single organ. It has been stated, for example, that the eye of the fruit-fly may be affected by more than fifty different genes.[7]

Riddle[8] has said: "Our stature, our facial features, the color of our eyes, skin and hair, the capacity of our blood to clot, our susceptibility to certain diseases and certain malformations of our bones and the nervous system, are all known to be influenced by genes. On the mental side, color blindness, feeblemindedness, some gradations of mental ability, and some forms of insanity are known to be influenced by genes." An interesting example of a type of idiocy with which there is an associated metabolic disturbance (the excretion of phenyl-pyruvic acid) has been studied by Penrose[9] and ascribed by him to a single recessive gene.

Some sixteen years ago, Riddle started an experiment to establish races of pigeons characterized by increased or decreased function of some of their endocrine glands. He started with twenty-four pair of birds taken from mongrel stock and bred them for fifteen generations, all the while selecting only individuals with particular types of glands for inbreeding. His most outstanding results were obtained in connection with the thyroid gland. He was able to produce three distinct strains or races, the individuals of each of which had a constant thyroid size, but the thyroid size was different in each of these races. But more important still, Riddle was able to show that the birds of different "endocrine" strain differed markedly in their basal metabolic rate, in body size, and in their degree of response to certain hormones injected into them. As Riddle remarks: "How much more valuable would such an experiment have been if it could have been done on human beings, because differences in behavior and in mentality could have been recorded." In any case, this most valuable contribution of Riddle shows unmistakably the great importance of genetic factors in relation to the development of the endocrine glands of each individual. Behavior, then, of the individual in so far as it is influenced by the endocrine glands is indirectly dependent upon the genes to which he has fallen heir and which, together with environmental forces, determine his endocrine constitution. This brings us to the constitutional factor which is so important in dealing with almost all human ailments, mental or physical. This is simply the expression of the combined results of the action of environmental influences and hereditary factors which have through their agents the genes made the individual what he is.

The studies of Smith and MacDowell[10] on the dwarf mouse furnish another excellent illustration of the effect of genetic factors on endocrine gland development. These authors have shown that a single gene controls the development of certain cells in the pituitary gland, and it is probable, when this gene is not present in the chromosomes of the mouse, that its pituitary gland cannot secrete certain of the active principles which the normal gland produces and liberates.

Environment is another important factor affecting endocrine activity. The hormones circulating in the blood constitute a part of the internal environment of living things. As pointed out earlier, the activity of the endocrine glands themselves may be affected by environmental factors and here the nervous system is often the channel used in communicating the stimulus arising in the external environment to the cells which produce the hormones. Blood-borne messages by means of chemical agents may also play a part here.

It is well recognized that environment can affect profoundly both physical and mental development, and hence behavior. Mendel was able to produce much larger rats by means of special diets; and, to borrow an analogy from the plant world, the growing soy-bean under red-yellow light will become a delicate twining vine; under blue-violet light it becomes a sturdy herb.[11] There are in the case of the human family cases of whole peoples showing behavior which we should judge as definitely abnormal, in whom as yet no evidence of abnormality, endocrine or otherwise, has been described. Examples such as paranoia in Dobu and the megalomania of the Kwakiutl must certainly be due in the main to the special environmental influences prevailing in each case — namely, the specific culture-patterns evolved by these societies. Yet, even in such societies as these, as in our own, there are doubtless differences of temperament and individuals who depart from the norm of the society in one direction or another; and it may well be that endocrine factors partly determine such individual variations. It may also be noted in this connection that even if the contention of the psychoanalysts be accepted that behavior traits in adult life are largely determined by the infant's solutions to the problems by which it is confronted — especially problems of nutrition, excretion, and sexual relationships — nevertheless, there is room in such theories for genetic factors, in part possibly endocrine, which in their turn determine which of the various possible solutions of these problems the child may finally accept.

While modern endocrinology was yet in the embryonic stage of development, the great French physiologist Claude Bernard pointed out that in all animals with complex organization, the living parts exist in the fluid which bathes them. He called this the *milieu interne*, the internal environment. Bernard recognized the great importance of the fixity of this internal environment as a condition for free and independent life. As Cannon has said: "The fluid matrix of the body is made and controlled by the organism itself." It is this ability of the higher forms of animal life to preserve uniform the composition of their tissue fluid that makes them more independent than their lowly ancestors of changes in the external environment. Many varied and complex physiological reactions together maintain the steady state of the internal environment. Such steady states which result from the coordination of various physiological processes have been described by Cannon as "physiological homeostasis." But in spite of the efficiency of the organization for homeostasis, changes of sufficient degree do occur at times in the internal environment to cause profound repercussions. Removal of an endocrine gland, for example, has an immediate effect on the internal environment, and in the period which follows, during which adjustment to the altered state is taking place, changes in many other organs may take place.

All tissues of the body are susceptible to slight changes in the composition of the fluid which bathes them, and this is particularly evident in the case of the more highly organized tissues such as the brain. Mind, from the biological viewpoint, may be considered as a function of the brain — its most recently acquired and highly evolved function. As a living tissue, the brain is particularly sensitive to changes in the internal environment. It follows, therefore, that the brain, the organ of mind, can be affected profoundly not only by changes in hormone content of the blood and tissue fluids to which the nerve cells are exposed, but by changes in any of the physical, chemical, or physiochemical properties of these fluids. Slight changes in subjective feelings, in thought, and in actions of normal individuals from month to month, from day to day, and even at times from hour to hour, may be logically explained as the result of the reactions of the higher centers to slight changes in the internal environment.

Summarizing, it may be said that behavior of the individual would seem to be determined by three things: (1) what he comes into life with — namely, his hereditary background; (2) his external environment; (3) his internal environment. It is only through this last channel that the direct effects of hormones on human behavior can be manifested. Indirectly, hereditary factors and the external environment can, as we have seen, produce changes in the hormone patterns of the internal environment. Thus each of these three can influence behavior indirectly through the hormones.

REFERENCES

1. R. G. Hoskins, *The Tides of Life* (W. W. Norton & Co., New York, 1933).

2. D. L. Thomson, in *Nature*, cxxx, 543 (Oct. 8, 1932).

3. L. F. Barker, in *Journal of the Florida Medical Association*, xiii, 254 (May 1927).

4. W. B. Cannon, *Bodily Changes in Pain, Hunger, Fear and Rage* (Appleton & Co., New York, 1915).

5. Harvey Cushing, *The Pituitary Body and Its Disorders* (J. B. Lippincott Co., Philadelphia, 1912).

6. A. W. Rowe, Collected papers from the Evans Memorial Hospital.

7. H. S. Jennings, *The Biological Basis of Human Nature* (W. W. Norton & Co., New York, 1930).

8. Oscar Riddle, Unpublished lecture, Cincinnati, 1936. Quoted by kind permission of the author.

9. L. S. Penrose, in *Lancet*, 1935, 1, 23.

10. P. E. Smith and E. C. MacDowell, in *Anatomical Record*, xlvi, 249 (Aug. 25, 1930).

11. H. W. Popp, in *Contributions from Boyce Thompson Institute for Plant Research*, 1 (1929), 241.

PRINCIPAL FACTORS DETERMINING INTELLECTUAL EVOLUTION FROM CHILDHOOD TO ADULT LIFE

JEAN PIAGET, DR. ÈS SCIENCES, LITT. D.

Professor of Child Psychology and of the History of Scientific Thought, University of Geneva

THE subject of our investigations is intellectual evolution — that is, the development of knowledge and of its different modes, the genesis of the forms of thought, of their adaptation to experience, and the rules which they obey.

In its point of departure this evolution raises a problem which is essentially biological; the relationship between understanding or perception and its objects is a particular case of adaptation — that is, a combination of assimilation and accommodation — which unites the organism with its external environment. The first question which the theory of the development of the understanding must investigate is how this relationship results from biological organization and adaptation. For example, it is impossible to determine how the elementary forms of spatial perception are evolved without seeing how they are related to the mode of inheritance of the organs of perception and of equilibrium, and to the different modes of organic adaptation.

But in the last analysis the evolution of individual thought is closely enmeshed in collective systems of knowledge, especially in those great systems of rational collaboration which deductive and experimental science has produced. The genetic theory of knowledge must therefore reach out into an historico-critical analysis of scientific thought, and also into genetic logic. For instance, to understand the evolution of the idea of space in the mind of a child, it is not enough to know how this idea is first born. One must also determine how the so-called "displacement groups" which form it follow one another in succession from the motor level to that of the most abstract conceptions; one must establish the respective parts of the scheme of logic and of the intuition in this formation; one must define exactly the relationship between the ideas of space and those of time, object, number, movement, speed, et cetera. In short, truly to understand the psychological aspect of the development of space, one must attack all the problems which this idea and related ideas suggest in the realm of mathematics and physics; but not from a point of view which is purely reflective and abstract, rather from one which is genetic and experimental. A comparative analysis must intervene between the psychological development of thought and the history of science.

The psychology of intellectual evolution leans therefore upon the biological theories of adaptation, the psychological theories of understanding, the sociological theories of signs and norms (the rules of socialized thought), the history of science, and upon comparative logic. One can then consider this special branch of psychology as a genetic theory of knowledge, a broad theory which must borrow its elements from a very great number of fields of research, thus partially synthesizing them, but withal an exact and well-defined theory, which has its own method, namely, the envisaging of intellectual realities only from the point of view of their development and genetic construction.

In fact, the best method for the psychological theory of the development of the understanding will always be the analysis of the intellectual evolution of the child. The thought of the child alone constitutes a continuous process which by a normal evolution links the initial sensorimotor adaptations to the socialized and scientific forms of understanding. In so far as the development of individual thought from birth to adult life can be observed directly and by experiment, and in so far as it is also open to the influences which various adult social groups have on the formation of the reason, this development forms an ideal field on which to set up all the biological, psychological, sociological, and logical problems of understanding in order to examine their genetic construction. A genetic and experimental epistemology is thus conceivable as a special branch of psychology.

We should like in what follows to give an example of this method and its results in studying — on the three planes of sensorimotor activity, egocentric thought, and rational thought — the genesis of some of those ideas of conservation (continuity) which play such a great role in scientific thought. As we trace this growth we shall also have the opportunity of following, on these three successive levels, the steps of one of the most important processes in the development of thought, namely, the passage from egocentric perception and thought to objective reasoning.

For the following hypotheses may be made in this matter. At the beginning of mental life, the world appears to the child as a series of pictures which are centered about activity and lack any intrinsic stability. The absence of permanent objects and of the objective organization of space seems thus to go hand in hand with a radical and unconscious egocentricity, so that the subject does not consider himself as one thing among many, but only conceives of things in relation to his own actions. Yet at the other extremity of the development the universe is considered as being formed of permanent objects whose movements take place in a space independent of us, and whose many relationships form a series of invariables which prolong the conservation of the object itself; invariables of number, quantity, matter, weight, et cetera. One may therefore say then that, in so far as egocentricity is reduced by the co-ordination of the individual point of view with other possible ones, the co-ordination which explains this reduction explains also the formation of logical instruments of conservation (ideas of "groups," systems of relations, et cetera) and the formation of invariables in the world of reality (ideas of the permanence of the object, of quantities, weights, et cetera).

I. *Sensorimotor Intelligence*

Even in the most elementary sensorimotor activities with which the intellectual development of the child begins, it is possible to discern certain of the processes of conservation. Because of the final richness of these processes, as well as their initial limitations, it is necessary to analyze them in detail.

It is evident that the reflex mechanisms (for example, sucking), the habits grafted on these reflexes (thumb sucking, et cetera), or the more complex "circular reactions" which tend to reproduce an interesting result (to swing suspended toys, et cetera) all lead essentially to repetition, and consequently imply a tendency toward persistence. On the one side these factors assume that movements are so organized that they are always capable of returning to their point of departure. From the point of view of space, these motor units form what the geometricians call "displacement groups," closed systems of operations which tend to continuance. On the other side, the elementary psychological activity which is characteristic of them is essentially an "assimilation" of external realities, so that these realities are not considered as entities in themselves, but only as functional elements (things are conceived merely as something to be sucked, something to be swung or handled, et cetera). Now this assimilation is also a factor in conservation, since it implies a certain practical recognition and a certain identifying generalization based on habitual repetition. Thus, when the baby of five or six months sees his usual rattle, or even a new plaything, dangling before him, he will swing it at once, assimilating it (by an assimilation which reproduces, recognizes, and generalizes) into the scheme of objects to be swung.

But, if these elementary sensorimotor organizations thus introduce from the very start a certain permanence into the primitive universe by constructing space in practical "groups" and by an assimilation of the things perceived into schemes of action, this conservation and this permanence emanate from the subject himself, and hence begin by presenting a purely egocentric character. In other words, there is not yet any conservation of objects as such, nor any permanence in the external world, not even in the space which forms its framework.

First of all, as far as objects are concerned, it is easy to establish the fact that, although the baby is capable of recognizing differences in things at a very early age, almost to the end of his first year he behaves as if the objects which disappeared from his field of perception momentarily ceased to exist. For instance, between the ages of five and eight months, when the child already knows enough to seize any solid objects which he sees, one has only to cover them with a cloth, or place a screen in front of them at the moment when the baby's hand is directed towards them, and he will give up looking for them and immediately lose his interest. I have even observed this in systematically hiding the bottle when my six months old son was about to take it. But one can see a still more curious reaction around nine or ten months, when the child is capable of seeking the object behind the screen and the notion of real exterior permanence begins to put in an appearance. For example, when the baby is placed between two pillows and he has succeeded in finding an object hidden under the right one, the object can be taken from his hands and placed under the left pillow before his very eyes, but he will look for it under the right pillow where he has already found it once before, as if the permanence of the objective were connected with the success of the former action, and not with a system of external displacements in space.

In short, the primitive world is not made up of permanent objects with autonomous trajectories, but of moving perceptive pictures which return periodically into non-existence and come back again as the functional result of the proper action. It is easy to prove still more clearly that this world is centered in the activity of the self by an analysis of the egocentric character of space which determines its configuration.

If the movements of the child are immediately capable of organization into "groups," closed and reversible systems, those "groups" are in the beginning centered entirely on the subject himself, and afford no room for any objective spatial construction. The clearest example of these egocentric "groups" is seen in the way in which a baby, before nine or ten months, rotates objects, a movement which finally forms the idea of the "wrong side" of objects. Every one has observed a child handling things and turning them over and over to explore their various sides. Now do these rotary movements give way immediately to the formation of objective groups? A very simple experiment shows us that this is not so. One has only to give a five or six months old baby his bottle with the nipple away from him, and turn it around slowly before his very eyes. If the child can see a bit of the rubber nipple at the other end of the bottle, he immediately turns the object around, but if he doesn't see the nipple, he doesn't even attempt to turn it, but sucks the wrong end! A series of other experiments with other "displacement groups" has shown the same centering on the subject and not on the object.

How then is the baby going to construct a world of permanent objects situated in a real space, and thus escape from his primitive egocentric universe? It is the work of the sensorimotor or practical intelligence, which precedes language, to set up a system of relations to co-ordinate this series of various perspectives which the baby has and thus cause him to locate himself among objects instead of illusively bringing them to him.

In other words, as the activity of the baby develops and the causal, temporal, and spatial sequences which this activity creates become more complex, objects are detached more and more from the action itself, and the body of the subject becomes one element among others in an ordered ensemble. Thus a total reversal of perspective takes place, which marks the beginning of the objectification of the external world, and of the idea of its permanence. The interplay of practical relationships in the world of reality teaches the child to shift the center of space and its objects from his action to himself, and thus locate himself at the middle point of this world which is being born. In this way the permanence of objects appears as the product of this formation of objective "groups" of displacements, and these groups themselves depend for their creation upon the way in which the sensorimotor or practical intelligence allows the child to free himself from his initial egocentricity and gives him power to act on things, thanks to a system of co-ordinated relationships.

But, if the co-ordination of practical relationships leads to a first victory over egocentricity and to the beginning of the objective idea of conservation, this external permanence remains limited to the plane of action and immediate perception, and cannot extend at once to the level of conceptual representation in general. In fact, it is in a sense an "ontological egocentricity" from which the practical intelligence delivers the individual, and not social and representative egocentricity, which will remain very important even after the appearance of language, and all through infancy. In other words, the co-ordination of practical relationships teaches the child that his body is one thing among many, and that he is thus part of a world of stable objects, whereas at the beginning the baby saw only a world of inconsistent pictures gravitating about his own activity. But the sensorimotor intelligence is not enough to teach the child that the perspective he has of this world is not absolute but relative, and must be co-ordinated with the perspectives of other people to attain a general and truly objective picture of reality.

II. *Egocentric Thought*

Just at the moment when the practical world of which we have been speaking has been created, the child comes into possession of language, and henceforth is called upon to adapt himself to the thoughts of others as well as to the external material world. Now on this new plane of thought which the social world creates, the child finds difficulties similar to those he has already overcome on the plane of the practical universe, and so he passes through stages similar to those of his escape from initial egocentricity and his progressive co-ordination. Hence the principles of conservation remain unchanged, only this time they are on the plane of abstract concepts. Although the child admits the permanence of concrete objects in the world of immediate experience, he really has no idea of the conservation of matter, weight, or movement, nor even any conception of logical or numerical groups. If he fails, it is because he lacks an intellectual instrument with which to construct the "invariables of groups" which are formed by physical realities. This instrument is called "the logic of relations" by the logicians, and is really the tool of co-ordination par excellence, both from the social and from the rational point of view. It is created only as it succeeds in stemming the egocentricity which constantly opposes it.

In order to make the link between the ontological egocentricity of the first sensorimotor stage and the social and logical egocentricity of the beginnings of conceptual thought perfectly clear, let us briefly turn again to the example of space. We have already seen that on the practical plane the child of two or three years is capable of using a certain number of "groups" of displacements: he knows how to turn an object over, to hide it behind one screen, or a series of two, and find it in the right place, et cetera. But what will happen when it is a question not only of acting upon the object, but of imagining distant objects, and of co-ordinating the perspective of different observers?

One of our assistants, Mlle. E. Meyer, has investigated this in the following experiment: the child is placed opposite a small model of three mountains, and given a certain number of colored pictures of these mountains; he is then asked which of the pictures show the mountains from the positions occupied successively by a doll on the moun-

tains in the model. The function of age in the development of these reactions is very clear. The little ones do
not understand that the observer sees the same mountains
quite differently from various points of view, and hence
they consider their own perspective absolute. But the
older ones gradually discover the relativity necessary to
objectivity, after a number of systematic errors due to the
difficulty of co-ordinating the relationships in question.
Here then on this social and logical plane of the co-ordination of perspectives we have a passing from egocentricity
to an objective "group" of changes, exactly parallel to
the passage one has observed on the sensorimotor level
in the relationships between the baby and the objects
handled, only this time the necessity of considering the
point of view of other people has created a new difficulty.

Now this process also influences very closely the idea of
the conservation or continuity of the mechanical and physical characteristics of objects as well as of their spatial
peculiarities. In fact, since the child considers a mountain
as being just what it appears to be in his own perspective, it
could not possibly have either form or stable dimensions—
that is, no "invariables of groups" are constructed. That
is actually what observation shows to be true. I have been
able to determine in experimenting on my own children, by
going about real mountains with them, that at about four
or five years of age they still considered the apparent
changes due to our own changes of position as quite real.
For every mountain they admitted the existence of changes
of form and dimensions absolutely contrary to the idea of
the permanence of objects. It would be easy to generalize
these results for all objects in distant space (stars, clouds,
et cetera).

But we must show how this preoccupation with the
problem of the proper perspective — that is to say, of "im-

mediate experience" as opposed to experience based on rational deduction — hinders the mind from co-ordinating relationships, and finally forming ideas of the permanence of matter, weight, movement, et cetera. It is clear that every principle of conservation implies a system of relationships which explains real permanence through apparent change. Now in so far as the mind is dominated by "immediate experience," it is not capable of recognizing this relativity, nor the "invariables" which it implies.

Here is an example dealing with the ideas of the conservation of matter and weight. We show children of different ages two paste balls of the same dimensions and weight. Then we change the shape of one of them to a cylinder (a sausage), and we ask if the two objects still have the same weight. Now the little ones think that the weight of the cylinder is less than that of the ball (because a ball appears to concentrate more matter in itself than an elongated cylinder), and they even state that the quantity of paste has diminished because of the change in form! But the older ones believe in the conservation of weight and matter; and between the two one finds a stage at which children think that weight alone varies with form, matter remaining constant.

In the same way, one of our pupils, Mlle. B. Inhelder, has shown that sugar dissolved in a glass of water is not conserved, in the minds of young children: the level which rises at the immersion of the sugar is considered as being lowered as before, after the sugar is dissolved; the sugar is conceived of as gradually vanishing, and even the sweet taste, which is all that remains of the dissolved piece, is supposed to disappear after several hours. But older children, by a series of steps it is useless to describe here, succeed in attaining the idea of the conservation of the sugar, its weight, and even the volume it occupied in the liquid. Some even go so far as to construct a kind of rude atomic theory, like that which the pre-Socratic physicists had, to account for these phenomena.

It is the same *a fortiori* in the case of more subtle ideas, such as that of the conservation of movement, or the principle of inertia. It is, indeed, easy to show that the physics of the child begins by being impregnated with an animistic dynamism, which is the direct opposite of the idea of inertia. Things are endowed with active forces, spontaneous and untransmittible, formed on the model of voluntary muscular activity. Later, before arriving at more mechanistic ideas, the child passes through an intermediate period which recalls in many respects the physics of Aristotle. Thus the trajectory of a projectile is explained, not by the conservation of the impulse received, but by an 'αντιπερίστασις in the real sense of the word, the projectile being pushed by the air it displaces in its progress. The clouds move in the same way, by the wind which their displacement arouses, et cetera.

It seems to us easy to show that all these ideas which are so contrary to the ideas of conservation are explained by the same causes, by an egocentric relationship, not yet reciprocal or rational, between the subject and the objects of the external world. On the one hand, objects are assimilated to the ego, and conceived on the model of its own activity. Hence the anthropocentric ideas of force, weight, et cetera, which are common in the physics of the little ones. On the other hand, experience remains "immediate," dominated by a series of successive impressions which have not yet been co-ordinated. It is not formed by that logic of relationships which alone will impress upon it an objective form by co-ordinating the many relationships which are perceived or conceived. Thus, in the case of the pellets which change their form, the child does not succeed in freeing his judgment from the illusions caused by habitual perceptions (we know the point at which the evaluations of weight are dependent on factors of form), that he may co-ordinate the relationships into a coherent ensemble which can support the deduction of real permanence. In short, the absence of permanence is the result of the pre-eminence of immediate experience over rational deduction, and immediate experience is the ensemble of subjective impressions, successively registered and not yet co-ordinated into a system of relationships which encloses the subject in an objective world.

III. *Rational Co-ordination*

We saw first of all how the sensorimotor co-ordinations led the child from an unstable world centered about his own activity to an idea of the permanence of objects, based on the formation of "displacement groups" which ordered space into an objective practical universe. On the other hand, we have just established the fact that when thought and abstract concepts are imposed on this sensorimotor world, egocentricity reappears on this new plane, and the world of concepts also begins to be centered in the ego, and is thus stripped of the basic permanence which reason demands. How is the child to surmount this second group of obstacles and reach the idea of rational permanence?

The process of reasoning on this plane of conceptual thought is exactly the same as on the sensorimotor level, with this difference, that it is a question henceforth of the co-ordination of the perspectives of different individuals, as well as the co-ordination of the different aspects of individual experience. This social co-ordination, which adds a new dimension to those which are already a part of rational co-ordination, creates in the intellectual realm what one might call "logic," in contrast to the sensorimotor or practical intelligence, which makes only perceptions and motions into systems. Logic is then the "group" of operations which co-ordinates the inter-individual relationships with the intra-individual ones into a system capable of assuring the permanence which is necessary to the invariables of experience.

The essence of rational co-ordination is then to be sought in the "logic of relations" — that is, in this fundamental group of operations which assures the reciprocity of individual perspectives and the relativity of the facts of experience. To refer again to the example of space, on which we have already insisted, it is the logic of relations which makes the child come gradually to understand, between seven and eleven years, that the left and the right are not absolute, but that his own left corresponds to the right of an individual opposite him, and that an object between two others is at one and the same time at the left of the first and the right of the third. It is then the logic of relationships which permits the formation of the idea of a conceptual space by the co-ordination of the different perspectives possible, and which also allows the imposition of this upon practical space, whose relationships, however well co-ordinated they may be among themselves, are always limited to one's own perspective.

Now this logic of relations, which thus maintains on the level of thought the "groups" of operations outlined by sensorimotor intelligence, and which gradually eliminates intellectual egocentricity, finally succeeds, in the realm we are trying to analyze here, in forming invariables which represent for the reasoning mind so many principles of permanence applicable to the physical world.

In the field of the permanence of quantity, for instance, it is easy to show how the grouping of relationships involves in each case the construction of formal invariables, which, when applied to reality, correct the illusions of non-permanence which we have just described in the "immediate experience" of infancy. In her investigations into the genesis of the ideas of quantity and number, our assistant, Mlle. A. Szeminska, brought to light a number of facts which make this change clear. Here are some of them.

When one fills a large glass with some continuous substance, such as colored water, or a discontinuous one, such as beads, and then separates these into two or four small glasses, or into some narrow and elongated or short and fat ones, et cetera, the quantities appear to increase or diminish for the child below seven years of age according to whether the subject considers the level of the substance in the receptacles, their size, or their number. Moreover, when one makes two groups correspond piece by piece (for example, the beads in two rectilinear rows), the child considers at first that the two quantities are equal; but this is only an illusion, because one has only to place the elements in one of these groups nearer or farther apart (to put the beads in a heap, or make one row longer and more widely spaced than the other) and the two quantities are no longer considered as equal; a row of ten beads is conceived as increasing in number if they are spaced more widely, and a pile is considered as containing more or fewer beads according to whether one heaps it up or spreads it out before the eyes of the child, et cetera.

In short, before the age of six or seven there is no idea of the permanence of continuous quantities, nor of discontinuous groups, nor any necessary equivalence between two groups which correspond piece by piece, et cetera, whatever the active operations may be which the subject himself performs in the course of the experiments. For this reason up to this age the child has not yet formed any idea of cardinal or ordinal numbers which are capable of indefinite extension; nor has he yet elaborated any idea of classes of things in extension, which depends upon the inclusion of parts in a permanent whole. The essential forms which number and logical class give to the mind are thus, after all, bound up closely with the processes of conservation, and one might say in general that if the thought of the child remains pre-logical during infancy, it is because of the lack of these very principles of permanence.

Now how does the child proceed from this pre-logical state to the discovery of the permanence of groups and quantities? By the co-ordination of the relationships involved; that is, by those operations of "multiplication of relations" which are essential to the logic of relationships. As soon as he ceases to envisage as separate unities the level, size, and number of the columns of liquid, the length of the rows, and the space between the objects, et cetera, the child succeeds in co-ordinating these relationships, in understanding their relative positions in a system of independent variables, and thus he forms units which are capable of permanence. It is therefore the logic of relationships which transforms immediate experience, with its illusions of perception, into a rational system, the changes of which depend on necessary invariables. It would be easy to show that the idea of the permanence of matter, weight, and movement, which we were speaking of above, is the result of similar processes. In the thought of the child, as in the evolution of the sciences, rational permanence always results from the union of a deduction based on the co-ordination of relationships with an experience similarly formed; and every invariable implies a "group" which creates it — that is, a system of related and reversible changes.

But you will say that the problem is not yet solved, that there still remains the question of how this "logic of relations" which explains the genesis of the principles of conservation and of the "invariables of groups" is itself originated. Now it is first necessary to understand the epistemological character of what we call the egocentricity of the child (i.e., a quite unconscious and natural illusion of perspective, which precedes moral egoism and conscious egocentricity). Then one will understand that this process of co-ordination, at once social and intellectual, by which the child escapes from his self-centered point of view to find his place among other people, is actually the rational instrument which makes up this logic of relations. For, in any field, the faculty of knowing is a process of co-ordination in which the ego is subordinated to some objective system of references, and the logic of relationships is nothing but a tool and a result of this co-ordination; a tool in that it guides the ego in its escape from itself, and a result since it is a grouping of systematic operations and an ensemble of successive invariables.

In conclusion, one sees how the genetic analysis of any aspect of the thought of a child necessarily corresponds to the analysis of scientific thought. Indeed, the effort by which the child, by means of that social and rational instrument which the logic of relationships gives him, escapes from his egocentricity and creates a universe is the very beginning of that ever-present gigantic effort of science to free man from himself by putting him within the relativity of the objective world.

PSYCHOLOGICAL FACTORS DETERMINING HUMAN BEHAVIOR

Charles Gustav Jung, M.D., LL.D., S.D.

*Professor of Analytic Psychology, Technische
Hochschule, Zurich*

THE separation of psychology from the premises of biology is purely artificial, because the human psyche lives in indissoluble union with the body. And since these biological premises hold good not only for man, but for the whole world of living beings, the scientific basis on which they rest obtains a validity far exceeding that underlying a psychological judgment, which is valid only in the realm of consciousness. Therefore it is not a matter of surprise that the psychologist is often prone to reach back to the security of the biological viewpoint, and to borrow freely from physiology and the theory of instinct. Nor is it astonishing to find a widely accepted point of view which regards psychology as merely a chapter in physiology. Although psychology rightly claims autonomy in its own special field of research, it is true that it must recognize a far-reaching correspondence between its facts and the data of biology.

Among the psychic factors determining human behavior, the instincts are primarily the motivating forces of psychic events. In view of the controversy which has raged around the nature of the instincts, I should like to establish clearly what seems to me to be the relation be-

tween the instincts and the psyche and why I name instincts as psychological factors. If we started with the hypothesis that the psyche is absolutely identical with the
state of being alive, then we should have to accept the
existence of a psychic function even in unicellular forms.
In that case, instinct would form a type of psychic organ
and the hormone-producing glandular activity would have
a psychic causality.

But if we look upon the appearance of the psyche as a
relatively recent event in evolutionary history, and assume
that the psychic function is a phenomenon accompanying
a nervous system, which in some way or other has become
centralized, then it would be difficult to believe that the
instincts were originally psychic in nature. And since the
connection of the psyche with the brain is a more probable
conjecture than the psychic nature of life in general, I regard the characteristic compulsoriness of the instincts as
an ecto-psychic factor. None the less, it is psychically important, because it leads to the formation of structures or
patterns, which may be regarded as determinants of human
behavior. Under these circumstances, the immediate,
determining factor is not the ecto-psychic instinct, but
that structure which results from the interaction of the
instinct and the psychic situation of the moment. Thus
the determining factor would be a modified instinct. The
change undergone by the instinct is as significant as the
differences between the color we see and the objective
wave-lengths producing it. The ecto-psychic fact of instinct would play the role of a stimulus merely, while the
psychic instinct-phenomenon would be an assimilation of
this stimulus to a pre-existing psychic complexus. A name
is needed for this process. I should term it psychification.
Thus, what we call instinct offhand would be a datum
already psychified, but of ecto-psychic origin.

I. *General Phenomenology*

The concept outlined above makes it possible to understand the variability of the instinctive factors within the general phenomenology. The psychified instinct forfeits its uniqueness to a certain extent, at times actually losing its most essential characteristic — compulsoriness; it is no longer an ecto-psychic, unequivocal fact, but has become instead a modification conditioned by its encounter with a psychic datum. As a determining factor, instinct is variable and therefore lends itself to different applications. Whatever the nature of the psyche may be, it is endowed with an extraordinary capacity for variation and transmutation.

For example, no matter how unequivocal the physical state of irritation called hunger may be, the psychic consequences resulting from it can be manifold. Not only can the reactions to ordinary hunger vary widely, but the hunger itself can appear as denatured, or even as metaphorical. It is not only that we use the word hunger in the most varied sense, but by combination with other factors, the hunger itself can assume the most varied forms. The originally simple and unequivocal determinant can appear transformed into pure greed, or into many aspects of boundless desire or insatiability, as for example, the lust for gain or inordinate ambition.

Hunger, as the characteristic expression of the urge to self-preservation, is without doubt one of the primary and most powerful factors influencing behavior; in fact, the lives of primitives are more affected by it, and more powerfully, than by sexuality. At this level of existence, hunger means the alpha and omega — existence itself.

The importance of the instinct of preservation of the species is obvious. However, the growth of culture having brought with it so many restrictions of a moral and a social nature, sexuality has been lent, temporarily at least, an excess value comparable to that of water in a desert. Because of the premium of intense sensuous enjoyment which nature has set upon the business of reproduction, the urge towards sexual satisfaction appears in man — no longer conditioned by a mating season — as an almost separate instinct. The sexual instinct enters into combination with many feelings and aspects, with spiritual and material interest, and to such a degree that, as is well known, the attempt has even been made to trace the whole of culture to these combinations.

Sexuality, like hunger, undergoes a radical psychification, which makes it possible for the primarily purely instinctive energy to be diverted from its biological applications and turned into other channels. The fact, that the energy can be deployed into various fields, indicates the existence of still other drives strong enough to change the direction of the sexual instinct and to deflect it, at least in part, from its immediate goal.

I should like, then, to differentiate as a third group of instincts the *drive to activity*. This urge functions when the other urges are satisfied — indeed, it is perhaps only called into being after this has occurred. Under the concept of activity would fall wanderlust, love of change, restlessness, and the play-instinct.

There is another drive, different from the instinct for activity and as far as we know specifically human, which might be called the reflection-urge. Ordinarily we do not think of "reflection" as ever having been instinctive, but associate it with a conscious state of mind. *Reflexio* means bending back and, used psychologically, would express the fact that the reflex process, which conducts the stimulus over into the instinctive discharge, is interrupted by psychification. Owing to the interference of reflection taken in this automatic sense, the psychic processes exert an attraction on the impulse-to-action excited by the stimulus. Therefore, before having discharged itself in the external world, the impulse is deflected into an endo-psychic activity. *Reflexio* is a turning inward with the result that instead of an immediate *act*, various derived contents or conditions result, which may be termed reflection or deliberation. Thus in place of the compulsive act, there appears a certain amount of freedom, and in place of the predictability a relative unpredictability as to the effect of the impulse.

The richness of the human psyche and its essential character are probably determined by this reflection-urge. Reflection re-enacts the process of excitation and conducts its stimulus over into a series of images, which, if the impetus is strong enough, is finally reproduced in some form of expression. This may take place directly, for instance in speech, or may appear in the form of abstract thought, of impersonations, of ethical conduct, or again, it may be expressed in a scientific achievement, or in a work of art.

Through the reflection-urge, this stimulus is more or less wholly transformed into psychic content, that is, it becomes an experience: a natural process is transformed into a conscious content. Reflection is the cultural instinct par excellence, and its strength is shown in the power of culture to maintain itself in the face of untamed nature.

Instincts are not creative in themselves, because they have been stably organized and have therefore become automatic. The reflection-urge is no exception to this rule, for the production of consciousness is not of itself a creative act, but may under certain conditions be a merely automatic process. It is a fact of great importance that this compulsion, so feared by civilized man, also produces that characteristic fear of becoming conscious, best observed in neurotic persons, but not in them alone.

Although in general instinct is a system of definitely organized tracks and consequently tends towards unlimited repetition, yet man has the distinctive power of creating something new in the real sense of the word, just as nature, in the course of long periods of time, succeeds in creating new forms. Though we cannot classify it with a high degree of accuracy, the creative instinct demands special mention. I do not know if "instinct" is the correct word. We use the term "creative instinct," because this factor behaves at least dynamically, like an instinct. Like instinct it is compulsive, but it is not common, and it is not a fixed and invariably inherited organization. Therefore I prefer to designate the creative impulse as a psychic factor similar in nature to instinct, having indeed a very close relationship to the instincts, but without being identical with any one of them. Its connections with sexuality are a much discussed problem, and, furthermore, it has much in common with the activity-urge as well as with the reflection-urge. Still it can repress all of these instincts, or make them serve it to the point of the self-destruction of the individual. Creation is as much destruction as construction.

To recapitulate, I emphasize the fact that from the psychological standpoint, five main groups of instinctive factors can be differentiated: hunger, sexuality, activity, reflection, and the creative. And in the last analysis, instincts are ecto-psychic determinants.

A discussion of the dynamic factors determining human behavior is obviously incomplete without mention of the will. The part that will plays, however, is a matter of dispute, and the whole problem is bound up with philosophical considerations, which in turn are burdened with the premises of a *Weltanschauung*. If the will is posited as free, then it is not bound to causation and there is nothing more to be said about it. If it is to be taken as predetermined and placed in a relationship of dependence upon the instincts, then it is an epiphenomenal factor of secondary importance.

Different from the dynamic factors are the modalities of the psychic function, which influence human behavior in other respects. Among these I mention especially the sex, age, and hereditary disposition of the individual. These three factors are taken first as physiological facts, but they are also psychological factors inasmuch as, like the instincts, they are subjected to psychification. Anatomical masculinity, for instance, is far from being proof of the psychic masculinity of the individual. And similarly, physiological age does not always correspond with the psychological. As regards hereditary disposition, the determining factor of race or family can be suppressed by a psychological superstructure. Much which is interpreted as heredity in the narrow sense is rather a sort of psychic contagion, which consists in an adaptation of the child-psyche to the unconscious of the parents.

To these three semi-physiological modalities, I should like to add three that are psychological. Among these I wish to stress the conscious and the unconscious. It makes a great deal of difference in the behavior of the individual, whether the psyche is functioning mainly consciously or unconsciously. Naturally it is only a question of a greater or lesser degree of consciousness, because total consciousness is empirically impossible. An extreme state of unconsciousness is characterized by the predominance of compulsive instinctive processes, the result of which is either uncontrolled inhibition, or a lack of inhibition throughout. The happenings within the psyche are then contradictory and take place in terms of alternating, a-logical antitheses.

In such a case, the level of consciousness is essentially that of the dream-state. In contrast to this, a high degree of consciousness is characterized by a heightened awareness, a preponderance of will, a directed, rational behavior, and an almost total absence of instinctive determinants. The unconscious is then found to be at a level definitely animal. The first state lacks intellectual and ethical accomplishment, the second naturalness.

The second modality is extraversion and introversion, and determines the direction of psychic activity, that is, it decides the question whether conscious contents refer to external objects or to the subject. Therefore, it also decides the question whether the value stressed lies without, or within the individual. This modality works so persistently that it builds up habitual attitudes, that is, types with recognizable external traits.

The third modality points, to use a metaphor, upward and downward, because it has to do with spirit and matter. It is true that matter is in general the subject of physics, but it is also a psychic quality, as the history of religion and philosophy clearly shows. And just as matter is finally to be conceived of as being merely a working hypothesis of physics, so also spirit, the subject of religion and philosophy, is a hypothetical quality in constant need of reinterpretation. The so-called reality of matter is attested in the first place by our sense-perceptions, while belief in the existence of the spirit is supported by psychic experience. Psychologically, we cannot establish anything more final with respect to either matter or spirit than the presence of certain conscious contents, some of which are labeled as having a material, and others a spiritual origin. In the consciousness of civilized peoples, it is true, there seems to exist a sharp division between the two qualities, but on the primitive level the boundaries become so blurred that matter often seems endowed with soul while spirit appears to be material. However, from the existence of these two categories, ethical, aesthetic, intellectual, social, and religious systems of values eventuate, which on occasion determine how the dynamic factors in the psyche are to be finally used. Perhaps it would not be too much to say that the most crucial problems of the individual and of society turn upon the way the psyche functions towards spirit and matter.

II. *Special Phenomenology*

Let us now turn to the special phenomenology. In the first part we have differentiated five principal groups of instincts and six modalities. However, the concepts described are only academically valuable as general categories. In reality, the psyche is a complicated interplay of all these factors. Moreover, in conformity with its peculiar structure, it shows an endless individual variability on the one hand, and on the other, an equally great capacity to undergo change and differentiation. The variability is conditioned by the circumstance that the psyche is not a homogeneous structure, but apparently consists of hereditary units only loosely bound together, and for this reason it shows a very marked tendency to split into parts. The tendency to change is conditioned by influences coming both from within and from without. Functionally speaking, these tendencies are closely related to each other.

1. Let us first turn to the question of the psyche's tendency to split. Although this peculiarity is most clearly observable in psychopathology, yet fundamentally it is a normal phenomenon, which can be recognized with greatest ease in the projections made by the primitive psyche. The tendency to split means that parts of the psyche detach themselves from consciousness to such an extent that

they not only appear foreign but also lead an autonomous life of their own. It need not be a question of hysterical multiple personality, or schizophrenic alterations in personality, but merely so-called complexes quite in the field of the normal. Complexes are psychic fragments, which owe their splitting off to traumatic influences or to certain incompatible tendencies. As the association experiment proves, the complexes interfere with the purposes of the will and disturb the performances of consciousness; they produce disturbances in memory and obstacles in the flow of associations; they appear and disappear according to their own laws; they obsess consciousness temporarily, or influence speech and action in an unconscious manner. In a word, complexes behave like independent beings, a fact especially evident in abnormal states of mind. In the voices heard by the insane, they even take on a personal ego-character like that of the spirits manifesting themselves through automatic writing and similar techniques. An intensification of the complex-phenomenon leads to morbid states, which are only more or less extensive multiple dissociations endowed with an invincible life of their own.

The behavior of new contents, which have been constellated in the unconscious, but are not yet assimilated to consciousness, is similar to that of the complexes. These contents may be based on subliminal perception, or they may be creative in character. Again, so long as they are not made conscious and integrated with the life of the personality, they also lead a life of their own. In the realm of artistic and religious phenomena, these contents likewise appear at times in personified form, especially as so-called archetypal figures. Mythological research designates them as "motives"; to Lévy-Bruhl they appear as *représentations collectives*; Hubert and Mauss call them "categories of fantasy." I have employed the concept of the collective unconscious to embrace all of these archetypes. They are psychic forms which, like the instincts, are common to all mankind, and therefore their presences can be proved wherever relevant literary documents have been preserved. As factors influencing human behavior, the archetypes play no small role. The total personality can be affected by them through a process of identification. This effect is best explained by the fact that the archetypes probably represent typical situations of life. Abundant proof of such identifications with archetypes is furnished by psychological and psycho-pathological cases. The psychology of Nietzsche's Zarathustra also furnishes a good example. The difference between these structures and the split-off products of schizophrenia lies in the fact that the former are entities endowed with personality and fraught with meaning, whereas the latter are only fragments with vestiges of meaning—in reality they are products of disintegration. Both, however, possess to a high degree the capacity of influencing, controlling, or even suppressing the ego-personality, so that a temporary or lasting transformation of personality occurs.

2. As we have seen, the inherent tendency of the psyche to split means on the one hand dissociation into multiple structural units, on the other, however, a possibility very favorable to change and differentiation: it allows the singling out of special parts in order to train them through concentration of the will and thus bring them to their maximum development. In this way, with a conscious one-sidedness, certain capabilities, especially those promising social usefulness, can be fostered to the neglect of others. This produces an unbalanced state similar to that caused by a dominant complex — a change in personality. It is true that we do not refer to this as obsession by a complex,

but as one-sidedness. Still, the actual state is approximately the same, with this difference, that the one-sidedness lies within the intention of the individual, and is therefore furthered by all possible means, whereas the complex is felt to be injurious and disturbing. Frequently one fails to see that the consciously-willed one-sidedness is one of the most important causes of an undesirable complex, or conversely, that certain complexes cause a one-sided differentiation of doubtful value. Some degree of one-sidedness is unavoidable and, in the same measure, complexes are also unavoidable. Looked at in this light, complexes might be identified with certain modified instincts. An instinct which has undergone too much psychification can revenge itself in the form of an autonomous complex. This is the chief source of the neuroses.

It is well known that very many faculties can become differentiated in man. I do not wish to lose myself in the details of case-histories and therefore limit myself to the normal and ever-present faculties of consciousness. Consciousness is primarily an organ of orientation in a world of outer and inner facts. First and foremost, consciousness establishes the fact that something is there. I call this faculty *sensation*. By this I do not mean any specific sense activity, but perception in general. Another faculty gives the interpretation of that which is perceived; this I term *thinking*. By means of this function, the thing perceived is assimilated and the transmutation of the object of perception into a psychic content proceeds much further than in mere sensation. A third faculty establishes the value of the object. This function of evaluation I call *feeling*. The pain or pleasure reaction of feeling marks the highest degree of subjectification of the object. Feeling brings subject and object into such close relationship that the subject must choose between acceptance and rejection.

These three functions would be quite sufficient for orientation with respect to any fact, if the object in question were isolated in time and space. But, in space, every object is in endless connection with the multiplicity of objects, and, in time, the object represents merely a transition from a former condition to the succeeding one. The greater part of spatial relationship and temporal change is unavoidably unconscious at the moment of orientation, and yet, for the determination of the meaning of an object, space-time relationships are necessary. It is the fourth faculty of consciousness, namely, *intuition*, which makes possible, at least approximately, the determination of the space-time relationship. This is a function of perception which includes the subliminal, that is, the possible relationship of objects not appearing in the field of vision, and the possible changes in past and future, about which the object itself gives no clue. Intuition is an immediate awareness of relationships which could not be established by the other three functions at the moment of orientation.

I mention the orientating functions of consciousness, because they can be singled out for empirical observation and are subject to differentiation. At the very outset, nature has established marked differences in their importance for different individuals. As a rule, one of the four functions is especially developed, which consequently gives the mentality as a whole its characteristic stamp. Through the predominance of one function there result typical dispositions, which can be designated as thinking types, feeling types, et cetera, as the case may be. Such a type-form is a bias like a vocation, with which a person has identified himself. Whatever has been erected into a principle or a virtue through inclination or usefulness always results in one-sidedness and a compulsion toward one-sidedness which excludes all other possibilities, and this applies to men of

will and action just as much as to those whose object in
life is the constant training of memory. Whatever we persist in excluding from conscious training and adaptation
necessarily remains in an untrained, undeveloped, infantile
or archaic state, ranging from partial to complete unconsciousness. Hence, together with the motives of consciousness and reason, unconscious influences of a primitive character are always normally present in ample measure and
disturb the attention of consciousness. For it is by no
means to be assumed that all those forms of activity latent
in the psyche, which are suppressed or neglected by the individual, are thereby robbed of their specific energy. For
instance, if a man relied wholly on the data of vision, this
would not mean that he would cease to hear. And if he
could be transplanted to a soundless world, he would in all
probability soon satisfy his desire of hearing by indulging
in auditory hallucinations.

The fact that the natural functions of the psyche cannot be stripped of their specific energy gives rise to characteristic antitheses, which can be best observed in the field
of activity where these four orientating functions of consciousness come into play. The chief contrasts are those
between thinking and feeling on the one hand, and between sensation and intuition on the other. The opposition between the first two is an old story and needs no
comment. The opposition between the second pair becomes clear when understood as the opposition between
the objective fact and the apparent possibility. Obviously
anyone on the lookout for new possibilities does not rest in
the actuality of the moment, but passes on beyond it as
soon as possible. These contrasts are marked by their irri-
tating nature, and this is equally true when the conflict
occurs within the individual psyche or between individuals
of opposite temperaments.

It is my belief that the problem of the opposites, here merely hinted at, should be made the basis of a critical psychology. A critique of this sort would be of utmost importance not only for the narrow field of psychology, but also for the wider field of the cultural sciences in general.

In this paper, I have gathered together all those factors which, from the standpoint of a purely empirical psychology, play a leading role in determining human behavior. The multiplicity and variety of the aspects claiming attention are due to the nature of the psyche — the mirroring of itself in many-sided facets — and they are a measure of the difficulties confronting the investigator. The tremendous intricacy of psychic phenomenology is borne in upon us only after we see that all attempts to formulate a comprehensive theory are foredoomed to failure. The premises are always far too simple. The psyche is the starting-point of all human experience, and all knowledge gained eventually leads back to it. The psyche is the beginning and the end of every realization. It is not only the object of its science, but the subject also. This lends psychology a unique place among all the other sciences: on the one hand there is a constant doubt as to the possibility of its being a science at all, while on the other, psychology gains the right to state a theoretical problem, the solution of which will be one of the most difficult tasks for a future philosophy.

In my survey, far too condensed, I fear, I have left unmentioned many illustrious names. Yet there is one which I should not like to omit. It is that of William James, whose psychological vision and pragmatic philosophy have more than once been my guides. It was his comprehensive mind which made me realize that the horizons of human psychology widen into the immeasurable.

PSYCHOLOGICAL STRENGTH AND WEAKNESS IN MENTAL DISEASES

Pierre Janet, M.D., Ph.D., S.D.

Professor of Psychology, Emeritus, Collège de France, Paris

I SHOULD like to address this assembly of men whose interests and studies are so widely diversified, who have come together to celebrate the long and brilliant life of Harvard University, on a general question which is of interest to observers in many fields, anatomists, physiologists, physicians, and psychologists.

I. *The Problem of Psychological Expression: The Psychology of Action*

Psychiatry, the science of mental diseases, finds one of its great difficulties in language. Because of the peculiar character of the phenomena that it studies, this discipline is obliged to use at one and the same time two different languages, and it continually sets them in opposition, mixes them, confuses them. First there is the *language of consciousness* used by the patient, which describes all the normal and pathological events which take place in the mind. This language has many advantages. It is rich and precise, it permits the delicate expression of all the feelings of the patient, and it is understood by pretty nearly everybody. But this language, quite different from that which is employed in other studies, permits no relationship between psychological facts and those described by anatomy or physiology. Furthermore, it is scarcely capable of quantified expression. Therefore, the observers who search for the organic conditions of mental troubles are led to use the *ordinary language of natural science* and the ordinary language of general medicine; the language of the perception of visual objects is much more scientific, much more susceptible of quantified expression, and permits indispensable correlations between the diseases of the mind and the other diseases of the organism, correlations which are necessary for the application of many forms of treatment. But this language is much more limited than the first, and has no words for the thousands of details which the patient wishes to express. Hence arise contradictions and misunderstandings: the medical anatomist and physiologist think the psychologist is a metaphysician and dreamer, the psychological observer thinks the anatomist a crude materialist, and science and the patient suffer.

Besides, different symptoms or groups of symptoms, perhaps because of these different languages, are described separately, independently of one another, and it is impossible to know exactly their relationship: a paralysis, an obsession, a delusional interpretation seem to have no relationship to each other, and in psychiatry there are no series of phenomena linked to one another by simple laws as there are in physics and chemistry. One finds only isolated descriptions, as in literature, where the language of consciousness throws into relief the diversity of feelings and thoughts rather than their similarity and unity.

Recently a Harvard professor, C. Macfie Campbell, in his splendid plea *Towards Mental Health* (1933), deplored the narrowness of our science of psychiatry, which deals only with the external disease as if it were some gross thing to be extracted from the body and does not concern itself with maintaining intact the internal status of the patient or the moral conditions of human life. This limitation of the study of the feelings, of personal frustrations, of religious compensations and illusions, has undoubtedly many causes. One of the most important of these seems to me to be the absence of a single language to express both the physical phenomena observed in the body from the outside and the internal and personal phenomena observed by consciousness.

Is it not possible to find a psychological hypothesis and a language which shall be somehow intermediate between the expression of the phenomena of consciousness and the observation of physiological phenomena? which shall permit the expression of both in the same tongue, and the establishment of useful relations between them? That is what we have tried to do in speaking of a *psychology of conduct*, and in attempting to classify normal or pathological mental phenomena from the point of view of *psychological strength and weakness*.

The general idea is that we ought to express all psychological facts in terms of actions, by words which designate the actions of the living being, and to look upon them as movements of the living being which determine modifications in the external world. These movements of living beings have special characteristics that distinguish them from the movements observed in purely material objects, in particular a certain novelty, an unexpected and unforeseeable quality, which constitutes vital adaptation. Among these actions must be included the movements of speech, which are an essential element of social adaptation in the adult man. This sort of psychology is a development of the psychology of *behavior*, so important in animal psychology. Such a psychology permits the expression of psychological phenomena in the language of visual and auditory perception adopted in all the other sciences.

It permits, more than one might think, the expression of

a very great number of psychological facts, especially if one considers those facts which the psychiatrist needs to know. First of all it expresses, of course, all the numerous actions that a man must perform under various circumstances. If we take into account the phases through which a tendency goes when it is activated, when it advances towards the terminal phase of the consummation of the act, the psychology of conduct allows us to describe the latent state of an action, the intention which is a phase of the evolution of the tendency, the intention, the desire, the effort, the very idea of the action, presented by Fouillée in his theory of the idea-force (*idée-force*) as the most common element in thought.[1] Feelings (*les sentiments*) are too often looked upon as irreducible elements of consciousness, or as simple physiological modifications; this is a very extreme view. Feelings are above all *regulations of action*, which action can be increased in strength, diminished, modified, or arrested in different ways.[2] Thought itself, from the psychiatric point of view, can be considered as one form of this action: it is an internal language due to the concealment of one's intentions and the adoption of secrecy (*l'acte du secret*).

We must not tarry indefinitely before the problem of consciousness, since the medical and practical point of view suffices for us. It is enough for us to be able clinically to distinguish between forms of conduct accompanied by consciousness and forms of conduct without consciousness; an epileptic attack, for instance, is not the same for us as a hysterical attack. In the one case the subject falls without any precautions, hurts himself, is placed in awkward, ridiculous, or dangerous situations; in the other case, the subject falls with care, avoids hurting himself and shocking those who are present. These differences can be expressed in the language of the psychology of conduct: we shall say that the epileptic has only reflex movements which are solely determined by external stimuli, and that the hysterical person supervises his actions, modifies them, regulates them. Consciousness will be presented as a reaction of the subject to his own actions, and that is enough for us in medical practice.

Undoubtedly the philosopher will not be quite satisfied: he will say that in the fact of consciousness there is a characteristic of specific quality which is not explained. Of course we do not pretend to account for the consciousness of blue or of red, of pain or of pleasure. This lack of knowledge is not complete and may be only temporary; there are qualities of this or that sensation which will become more and more precise and which will be able to indicate at least the distinguishing marks of this or that sensation. The philosopher will say quite rightly that there is in the act of the living being something specific which sets it apart from a material movement, that there is already in this act an adaptation, a thought; and he will attribute to the action at its starting point a characteristic analogous to that which we observe in its most advanced stages. There is some danger in this procedure, and perhaps it is not quite justifiable to place something at the origin of a development which we observe at its completion. But that matters little, for psychology is willing to admit the specific and in part irreducible character of the object of its studies, and does not pretend to explain everything. All science stops at a certain point; neither chemistry nor physics explains the nature of the atom, the electron, or the neutron; they do not explain the real nature of a vibration of the ether. After the investigations of psychology there will remain many mysteries the study of which will be reserved for general philosophy, and psychology will confine itself to delimiting its sphere without claiming to be metaphysics.

This study of action allows us to make a beginning in the quantitative analysis of psychological phenomena, for actions differ from one another and can be classified to a certain extent in a hierarchical system. It is obvious that a reptile does not behave like a monkey, and that a new-born babe does not perform the same acts as an adult man. There are simple actions like the first reflexes of the sucking infant, and much more complex actions such as beliefs and criticism of beliefs. These various actions have originated at different times; the older ones are the most fixed and the easiest, the more recent ones, which are still in the process of formation, are variable and difficult. It is important to characterize a man by the actions which he can most frequently accomplish; there are low-tension forms of behavior which consist only of actions of the first degree, and high-tension forms which consist of actions on a higher level. The oscillations of the mind which passes from one level of tension to another play a great role in all mental troubles. This is indeed only a psychological expression of the very important principles established by the great English physiologist Sherrington with regard to the functions of the nervous system being imposed one upon another. But it is important to set up a hierarchical table of this sort in the description of actions from the point of view of psychology.

Unfortunately this first classification is not enough, because the capacity to carry out actions of a superior type is very variable even in the same individual, and depends on a host of circumstances. Let us take for example an operation on a fairly high level, the act of discussion. An individual is capable of discussion: he has his own opinion and does not share that of his interlocutor; he wishes to resist with valid arguments. We observe that he argues correctly for a certain length of time, then ceases to answer and seems to accept the opinion of his adversary. Yet he is not convinced, and continues to maintain his own belief, but he acts now as though he accepted the other thesis; he either knows no more, or can no longer defend himself. This momentary cessation of discussion plays a role in the phenomenon of suggestion.

I have recently made a fairly common observation. A young woman of thirty, six weeks after confinement, developed a puerperal psychosis, with a state of mental confusion and a dream-like delirium which lasted two months. She recovered consciousness, became clear, and began to talk coherently. She can talk quite charmingly and intelligently for a quarter of an hour, but then her gaze becomes clouded; she answers more slowly and irrelevantly, and if I continue to talk with her the delirium returns. If she is left alone for an hour she can again talk intelligently.

For the living being different actions are not all equally easy to carry out: they bring about modifications, reductions of tension which render renewed performance of superior actions impossible. There are expensive actions and inexpensive actions, depending on whether their performance can be prolonged for a shorter or longer time without inducing changes in behavior. This idea is allied with the preceding one concerning the hierarchy of actions, since it is easy to see that the highest actions in the psychological hierarchy are the most costly, and the lowest the most economical. The evoking of words or actions by automatic association is easy, it does not induce any change in the mind, and we shall call it inexpensive; the considered evoking of ideas adapted to a new situation, and above all the adaptation involved in the various forms of social behavior, are difficult and much more expensive.

Observations of this sort are very numerous and varied; we cannot examine them thoroughly today, but it is our aim to summarize them by a general hypothesis which is of help to us in the diagnosis and treatment of patients. In the realm of the mind there are psychological expenditures and profits; I would even go further and say that there are psychological savings, loans, and debts. It is very often useful in psychological language to employ expressions borrowed from the language of finance. Nothing is more psychological than the bank, and a day will come when the study of financial problems and even of political problems will form chapters in treatises on psychology.

The hypothesis, or, if you prefer it, the verbal formula which these facts lead us to adopt, is that things take place as if there existed in each individual a given quantity of a particular force, which is expended in costly actions, which is restored in sleep and in inexpensive actions, and which we can agree to call *psychological force*. This expression is already used continually in everyday language, which even from the ethical point of view refers to the weak and the strong, admits moral weaknesses and strengths, and speaks of moral exhaustion and of recuperation of mental forces. But this is popular language, to which we must give a more exact meaning when we take the dynamic point of view in the study of human behavior.

To attain this goal the psychologist must act like the physicist who talks of electric force without involving himself in too many premature interpretations of its final nature, limiting himself to observing and measuring its various manifestations when that is possible. Psychological force should not too quickly be confused with vital force, with spiritual force. The former term should designate only certain properties of action — its power, its speed, its duration in relation to its degree of perfection, or its psychological tension. In the neuroses and the psychoses one should study the dynamic aspect of actions, the expenditures in costly actions, the resources of the organism, and the necessary balance between expenses and receipts.

II. *Psychological Asthenias*

It is useless to insist here on these general considerations; it is better to show the application of these ideas about psychological force in the interpretation of a very widespread disorder, the point of departure of many mental troubles; I refer to *psychological weakness*.

This notion of a certain weakness in behavior is already very old. It is found in all the theories on the neuroses so often presented by the early disciples of "animal magnetism." It is contained in the teachings of Beard in 1880 on neurasthenia, and is still well known under his name of *nervous exhaustion*. Likewise it was well explained by Hack Tuke between 1872 and 1886. I believe that in 1903 I defined somewhat more exactly this all-too-vague concept in my studies on the psychasthenic,[3] which described a rather special form of this asthenia in neuropathic patients with obsessions and phobias. There are more general studies by Déjerine and Gauckler, and especially by Deschamps in his book on asthenias in 1909. Since then several authors have studied particular forms of this trouble and I shall mention the names of Manouvrier, Tastevin, Couchoud, Iscovesco, R. Bénon, and the report of Adrian to the congress at Oxford in 1926 — works which I believe I summarized and supplemented in my lectures on *Psychological Force and Weakness*.[4]

First of all, one must not confuse psychological asthenia with intellectual defect: the intellect properly speaking, characterized by its abundance of possible acts and by its ability to organize new acts which are intermediate between fixed patterns of action of ancient origin, is not the same as *psychological force*.[5] The great development of the intellect is far from being favorable to the development of psychological force. It seems indeed that the extension and spreading of this force over a large number of actions reduces its strength in a particular act, and the great intellectuals can be asthenics. The value of a man can be measured by his capacity to accept unpleasant tasks, and the most intelligent men are not always those who accept them most readily. Inversely, people who are intellectually debilitated and whose intellectual activity is of narrow range may have considerable psychological strength. Nor must one confuse psychological asthenia with purely physical weakness, although sometimes it accompanies the latter. Muscular and robust individuals can be psychological asthenics, and there are even cases where violent muscular discharges in maniacal states and other psychotic episodes can be the expression of great psychological asthenia.

We also pass over for the moment visceral symptoms, a great number of physiological troubles, certain forms of headache, of asthma, of urticaria, of gastro-intestinal disturbance, which are often, more than one would think, connected with asthenia. It is commonly said that these are troubles of the sympathetic system, but the latter is dependent on the cerebral functions and subject to repercussion from all disturbances of the psychological force. When a fortune is greatly diminished the resources which remain can be distributed in many ways; some people cut down all their expenses equally, others reduce in too drastic a way certain expenditures — such as those for food or the upkeep of their dwelling — and devote their entire resources to dress and external luxury. One can say in certain cases that the reduction of activity has most effect on the visceral functions. But we have to consider above all the disturbances which this weakness induces in conduct.

Psychological asthenia manifests itself in symptoms

which may be called direct and immediate, and which are connected with the reduction of force, and in indirect symptoms which are in a more or less complicated way the result of the former. The immediate symptoms are above all the disappearance or reduction of those actions which ordinarily occur under the circumstances in a normal man. It is not a question of the disappearance of the possibility of these actions, of the destruction of the tendencies and organs upon which these actions depend. One is surprised to discover that under certain conditions which cannot always be exactly defined these actions, suppressed for a long time, reappear in an unexpected way. This is the case with patients who for a long period seem incapable of walking, talking, or observing things, and yet for several minutes walk or talk well and show that they have made delicate observations, of which they had been thought incapable. As I usually say, it is like a machine, an automobile with a perfect mechanism which does not function because the gasoline tank is empty.

The various components of the action are affected unequally. Patients become incapable of beginning an action, they have no initiative; they wait until someone prompts or commands them to do something because of themselves they would do absolutely nothing. They find as much difficulty in commencing to entertain themselves as in commencing to work: someone else must amuse them, and, whatever the action may be, they are hard to get started.

When they have begun some action, they sometimes exhibit a certain precipitation because they are in a hurry to be through with it; but most often they act very slowly. This slowness is sometimes related to various obsessions or various scruples, but at its starting point it is due to their weakness. Let us not forget that they are just as incapable of finishing something as of starting it; sometimes they continue the action indefinitely without noticing that it is no longer of any use, but most often they stop before they have finished. We have often watched a kitten playing with a ball with magnificent eagerness, and have seen it stop all at once and fall asleep, as if the gasoline tank had suddenly become empty. A sick woman in a very characteristic state once said to me: "I cannot read another line or take another stitch; I feel a sudden stop in my forehead and I need at least a half hour of being absolutely motionless before I can begin anything again. No one can do anything for me; it is a complete impotence in which everything is wiped out; everything stops — I am a butterfly whose wings have been clipped."

A normal individual continues an action which he has begun and he arrives at its consummation, although the reserve of the tendency which corresponds to this action be exhausted; he supplements this deficiency in the tendency by force supplied through effort. Effort consists in adding to the tendency in play the forces maintained in reserve in some other tendency which is evoked in its turn. The child who no longer has a desire to read reads on, if he is promised some bread and jam. Now there is an important reserve of energy in the tendencies which are organized around the habitual actions of the personality; it is the energy in these tendencies and their maintenance in activity which permits the consummation of the act through effort.

The outstanding characteristic of asthenics is that they are incapable of summoning up energy and maintaining it on a given subject: Ribot had already observed their inclination to put forth the least effort possible.[6] The patients seem active when they limit themselves to expending the energy of a tendency, which, quite by accident, is strong in them. They carry out zealously what pleases them, whatever is natural to them; but if the tendencies in question do not exist in them, or if their energy is exhausted, their activity ceases without the effort of the personality being able to continue it. While effort may exist for a moment, it is quickly exhausted, and instinctively the patient casts about for rapid actions which can be consummated before the end of this little reserve of effort is reached. "The degenerate, the morally insane of every sort, criminals and prostitutes live by cunning at the expense of others or by a violent effort exerted all at one time." [7]

There is one detail of these states of exhaustion, of these stoppages of effort, which seems to me of great importance from a clinical standpoint, that is the phenomenon of discharge so characteristic of states of asthenia. An example will indicate clearly the nature of this phenomenon; we find it in a little experiment which is not without value in diagnosing that chronic and progressive asthenia which constitutes *dementia praecox*. The doctor asks the patient to perform a trivial act, for example to write his name and address. Sometimes the patient acquiesces and is very co-operative, but he seems uneasy and preoccupied by the difficulty of the action requested. He begins and writes a few letters with a noticeable effort; then all of a sudden he stops, lets the pencil fall, and bursts into laughter. After this laughter he refrains from all effort, appears to have forgotten utterly the action demanded of him, which he had begun, and is visibly much more at ease. This laughter of the patient with dementia praecox, characteristic of severe asthenia, is a discharge of the energies, trifling but actual, which had been mobilized for the action and which the patient is incapable of maintaining in a condition of mobilization while gradually expending them.

Discharges of this type having the same meaning can

take extremely varied forms. They will be made up of grimaces, twitching, vile language, frequent bursts of anger, masturbation, anxiety, cramps or convulsive movements of various kinds; the most important of these discharges occur in the convulsive attacks of epilepsy and hysteria. Nothing is more interesting from the point of view of the study of psychological forces than the analysis of the mental state of the epileptic; a patient examined before and after the attack shows the most extraordinary oscillations of psychological forces. These forces increase in the period which precedes the attack, and it is at the moment when the subject appears to have gained the most energy that he falls in tonic convulsions. That is what the disease is: the inability on the part of the patient to maintain his forces at this high degree of tension, and the necessity of releasing them. After the attack he is depressed and even shows melancholic states of various degrees. These observations show us that the releasing of forces plays a part in many agitated states. In the period before the attack, when these forces, which are already getting beyond control, are accumulating, we see—even in the case of the epileptic—obsessions, maniacal agitation, feelings of very great well-being which border on the ecstatic; after the attack we observe feelings of sadness and even ideas of persecution.

All these disturbances that are due to the discharge of forces raise the highly important question of the *mobilization of forces* and of their maintenance in this state for a comparatively long time. Psychological forces are ordinarily latent, held in reserve; but once they have been mobilized by the awakening of the tendency they tend to expend themselves immediately in action. They are controlled and utilized progressively in high-tension actions which absorb and organize many component forces. As I

have tried to show, in order to act calmly one must preserve *a certain proportion between the psychological force and
the tension.*[8] When the tension cannot be maintained on a
high level because the maintenance is too costly, the forces
which have been mobilized and insufficiently used in high-
tension acts expend themselves rapidly and crudely in actions of a lower order and even in quite primitive movements such as the reflex movements of the epileptic fit.

There are certain weak individuals who are unable to
maintain a certain tension and to support the mobilization
of psychological forces, and who have distressing or dangerous states of agitation as soon as they have at their disposition a greater accumulation of energy. Tonics, even
sleep, may only increase their agony and the accidents
which befall them. Inversely it is surprising that periods
of great weakness in the course of serious illnesses, of convalescence, or even of intoxication through sedative drugs,
bring about the relief of the most distressing disorders. It
is known that epileptics are free from attacks during pneu-
monia or typhoid fever, and that bromide and gardenal
suppress the attacks by reducing the reserve of forces
which can be used; the same may be said in regard to
obsessions. Due proportion between the psychological
tension and the psychological forces must always be maintained in order to remedy what I have elsewhere called
the paradoxes of agitation.

I have insisted on this phenomenon of discharge because
it is an essential characteristic of asthenics who have not
yet found their psychological equilibrium, and because it is
an essential element in a large number of disturbances in
which agitation is combined with asthenia.

The group of psychological anomalies which I have been
discussing often appear under the aspect of *laziness.* For a
long time laziness was thought to be a moral fault. It is

only recently that we have understood its pathological character. One recalls the amusing book by M. Laumonier, *Les sept péchés capitaux* (1922), in which he presents the pathological side of these deadly sins, and shows that laziness is a kind of mental disorder.

To understand this statement one must recall the ideas of psychology about *work*. We all work today, but this work is far from being a primitive psychological reaction. An animal which, as I have said, has not memory as does man, can no more have work: horses do not work; they are forced to perform an act which externally resembles our work.[9] Each tendency at its formation has its own reserve of force, and it is this reserve force which the animal expends in his action. Man adds to this the force of effort which is borrowed from other tendencies. He has invented work by transforming this activity, perfected by effort, into a new tendency. Work came into being at the same time as rational and moral behavior, and we have acquired the singular habit of working all the time. This is the factor which has formed civilized nations, differentiated thereby not only from animals but also from many half-civilized peoples who hardly know what work is.

The conclusion is that work is a higher psychological function, demanding psychological tension, reserves of energy, and the ability to exert habitual effort. That is why one of the first symptoms of asthenic depression is the cessation of professional work: professional obsessions, phobias, aboulias, are quite characteristic phenomena. Like Féré in 1887, many authors have insisted on this inability to work in some individuals. But asthenia can occur in the form of incidental depression, and for a certain time it suppresses all work and all effort. The patient seems calm when he is lying down and quiet and has nothing to do, but if one attempts to urge him to do something he becomes immediately agitated and distressed: "I haven't even the energy to say 'No.' The very thought of making an effort puts me into a cold sweat."

What is particularly important and unfortunate is the constitutional laziness as a result of asthenia which develops in some children in our countries, and which occasions many serious pedagogical errors. I have seen children who were hereditary constitutional asthenics commit suicide, misunderstood and martyred by their parents and teachers. These are children who unfortunately for themselves appear intelligent and capable, but whose family is in despair because it always receives the same characteristic report from the teachers: "The child is intelligent, but doesn't do what he can." This formula seems banal, but it is very profound and exact. The child is intelligent because he has all the psychological faculties, their activity is apparent from time to time when they are spontaneously aroused; but he does nothing for the teacher since he never adds the accessory impulse of effort to these faculties. It is this contradiction not understood which brings about family scenes. Knowledge of this pathological laziness is one of the most important results of these studies of psychological asthenia.

Another general characteristic of this group should be pointed out: this is *instability*. The victims of asthenia not only fail to persevere in any action, but they are able to maintain interest in the same object for only a brief period, and they seem constantly to change their activity and their tastes. That is the reason why certain individuals change their studies or their occupation so frequently. I have seen some who have begun and subsequently abandoned seven careers and seven different kinds of examinations. They decided on a program, enthusiastically began their preparation, and then after several weeks became quite disgusted with their work and felt the need of taking up some other kind of study. Such people are capable of finishing nothing, no more the reading of a book than a student's task or even a game.

This instability is also found in the realm of the feelings. These individuals appear to love one person very much, and then become tired of that person, hate him, and pass on to another. I have seen sick girls oscillate in the most curious fashion between mother and nurse, loving and hating first one then the other in turn.

The degree of psychological tension oscillates in the same way. Sometimes it rises, and this brings on a discharge, perhaps in the form of convulsions, perhaps as a sick headache, which is often the equivalent of a hysterical attack; sometimes the tension is lowered after the discharge; and the doctor should be informed of these changes, because he is not always dealing with the same individual. Oscillations of this type seem to me to grow less with age, because the patient often becomes fixed at a lower level, and as he no longer rises as high as before, he has fewer falls, that is discharges. This instability and these variations are a manifestation of the weakness itself: the energy associated with a tendency or with some slight effort is quickly exhausted or vanishes in a discharge, and there must be a change to another tendency or to another feeling before a certain degree of function can return.

III. *The Systematization of Asthenias*

In order to diagnose these asthenias and appreciate their importance we must not forget the propensity of the mind toward functional systematizations. Although asthenia is most often a general disorder of conduct, it must be remembered that it may to a predominating degree bear on certain groups of actions. We already know that asthenia more easily affects superior functions of high tension which concentrate a greater quantity of energy in a single act. One must add that it suppresses more quickly acts of initiative which require a new organization; instinctive, habitual actions, automatic acts, even when they are impulsive, persist very much longer, as Billod (1847) and Ribot (1883) had already pointed out in their studies on *diseases of the will.*

An important detail is the activity of thought in the form of internal language, a limited activity which is much less expensive than motor activity. This secret activity is not exposed to the discussion and criticism of other men. It is safe to relax one's surveillance of it to some extent: it is less precise, ideas may remain vague, may be indefinitely repeated, and may contain all kinds of absurdities, since it is not necessary to transform them into actions or to submit them to the judgment of others. Our patients cherish and love this reverie, which even provides them with a slight stimulation, and they seem to take refuge in it. This propensity has often been treated as a separate symptom under the name of *autism.* But one must not exaggerate its importance, because it is only one of a number of manifestations of psychological asthenia. If the patients misuse reverie, it is not through deliberate choice, but often because they cannot do otherwise. As asthenia increases still more, the patients lose even the resource of reverie, which first begins to lose its charm and then disappears more or less completely. But the disappearance of autism is far from being always a sign of progress; it may indicate decline.

I have had occasion to note more curious systematizations, sensorial systematizations. A young man of twenty, who is a case of severe constitutional asthenia, shows an especial weakness of the visual functions. Although his eyes are normal, especially if examined quickly, this young man soon develops asthenopia and even strabismus and transitory diplopia if he tries to look at anything for a long time. In this context I wish to mention the pains which he feels in the neck muscles, especially at their cranial insertion. These muscles play a large role in ocular fixation and perhaps their fatigue plays some part in the occipital pains which are so common among these patients. Another subject complains especially of these same pains and asthenopia when he tries to look sideways and can only look straight ahead. I was especially interested to learn that the first patient can perform no intellectual operation which requires the use of his eyes as a starting point. He cannot understand or learn a lesson if he has to read it himself. He has the singular habit of asking some obliging comrade to read his lessons aloud to him several times. In this way he can learn a lesson which is read to him and which he hears, whereas it is impossible if he reads it himself.

Finally there is a systematization of psychological asthenia to which I attach the greatest importance, that which bears upon the social psychological functions. One sees it develop in many of our cases in childhood in the form of disturbances of family feeling. From infancy asthenics adapt themselves poorly to family life. The young man whose visual weakness I have just mentioned always hated his father, who did not understand him at all; "he did not love his mother who criticized everything severely and did not know how to comfort him; he was disgusted with his brother who was constantly acting so as to show off his superiority."

In adolescence and youth there occur disorders due to timidity to which, in my opinion, we do not attach enough importance. Our patients suffer horribly if they have to attend some social gathering, they easily develop a morbid fear of blushing, are morbidly apprehensive because of a little pimple on the nose which will make them ridiculous. They have often told me of their well-known and characteristic dream of a desert island. "They would be cured immediately, they would be supremely happy, if they could live on a desert island without any other human being near them." One intelligent young girl was willing to have a colored servant with her on her desert isle to cook good meals, but only on condition that she be dressed in a red and green cloth and, most important of all, be deaf and dumb. This showed well enough what it was she feared in social life.

These patients realize more than might be supposed their dreams of the desert island, because there is one important fact which is a characteristic symptom. They have no friends, although they claim always to have desired intimate friendships. They have not known how to acquire friends, or to keep those whom they had for a short time in their childhood when their social asthenia was not yet complete. The friends they claim to have are imaginary ones they have created in their inner reveries, and whom they place on earth or in heaven. These are not the real friends with real differences of character and situation who create social difficulties.

Hence what difficulties, what disappointments, what mental troubles — in connection with marriages, with professional relations, with social groups which are either too complex or are badly formed! Finally, what a sad ending for many neuropathic troubles, which too often terminate in delusions of persecution! The various feelings of influence which characterize persecutory states express the feeling of the difficulty of social action of the asthenic.

Timidity, which is the starting point for all these

troubles, is not, as has too often been said, a disease of the emotions. The attack of timidity is quite secondary, it is a discharge connected with the social inadequacies, which are the fundamental factors and of much longer duration. These patients are first and foremost social weaklings, incapable of correctly carrying out the simplest social acts of imitation, of command, or of obedience. They do not know how to talk with another person, or to express their opinion or defend it; they do not know how to act upon another person, to arouse him, or to let themselves be stirred by him; they are unable to understand the simplest habits of politeness. A man of this type, already forty and living in good society, told me that he was very much afraid of having friends who might lay terrible obligations upon him, such as having to send cards of congratulation or condolence. "It exhausts me to see people," another told me; "I keep the bit of brain I have for myself, and I don't like to squander it in discussion and useless words. I want to be able to talk by myself without having to be on my guard against indiscreet or foolish utterances."

These reflections of our patients are not false, because these people really encounter great difficulties in social life. The social act is always a complicated one. It consists not alone of our own action, but also of the representation of the act of the socius which will be a reaction to ours; this is clearly apparent in an analysis of jealousy and of sympathy, and especially in the analysis of those actions of command and obedience which are so fundamental in social life. These actions are further complicated by language which combines and evokes in a single phrase the representations of a very large number of actions. The difficulty of social life is increased still more by the necessity of establishing the serious relationships of inferior and superior among men, when one must face the conflicts involved in attaining social value. Hence there is nothing more difficult and fundamentally more expensive than one's conduct in a group of acquaintances, relatives, husbands and wives, children, and friends who try not only to act in common, to struggle for their places in the social hierarchy, but also to mold one another, to bring about a satisfying interplay of feeling, excitants which help them to live.

Undoubtedly in some cases certain forms of sexual conduct add considerably to psychological expenditure, as the philosophers and the clinicians have long since demonstrated, but these forms of sexual conduct must not be exaggerated and considered separately, as if they were the determining factors in all the difficulties of social life. Often the difficulties of sexual conduct are dependent upon preceding complications and do not create them; they only add one more element of trouble. When subjects already show forms of psychological asthenia, the expenses in these social acts are really ruinous and are the cause of many troubles and justified fears.

This localization of asthenia in the social functions can be hereditary, but it also depends to a large extent upon the situation of the family and upon training. To understand the development of the mind one must consider the social conditions prevailing during childhood, for there is a psychology of wealth, and there is a psychology of poverty. The rich child, accustomed from earliest infancy to being shown off in the drawing room, to receiving many comrades, and to being received by them, develops the social functions quite differently from the child who has always been poor and has lived in isolation and obscurity. There are many other circumstances in addition to this one, but in all sorts of ways the systematization of asthenia in relation to the social life plays a large part in the evolution of delusional states.

IV. *Reactions to Psychological Asthenia*

To this first group of symptoms, which may be considered as the immediate expression of the reduction of the psychological forces, is to be added a considerable body of facts which are more or less indirectly connected with this same psychological asthenia. These troubles are determined by various reactions provoked by asthenia, reactions which are so common that they form, so to speak, a part of the habits of every individual who is weakened in this way for any length of time.

One of the most frequent results of psychological asthenia seems to me to be the propensity toward various kinds of obsessions. The patients seem to suffer from a kind of forced activity, imposed upon them in spite of themselves, which urges them to repeat indefinitely certain physical or intellectual actions, to ask perpetually the same question, to count, to discuss the same moral, philosophical, or religious problem with endless rumination, without the power to stop.

This forced labor depends first of all to a great extent on the earlier asthenia which is felt and appreciated in a more or less clear fashion in various feelings of incompleteness. In my first studies on obsessions [10] I laid much stress on the importance of these feelings of weakness, but today I no longer believe that this interpretation is enough. The objection I make to my own theories is that in indubitable and serious cases of asthenia obsession may be entirely absent. The observation of the following case seems to me a very good demonstration of this point.

For forty years Lise, whom I studied in detail in my book on the obsessions, was a case of severe obsession, but in observing her I have noted two strange facts. She had to undergo a serious surgical operation, the removal of the gall bladder; her convalescence was very difficult; she was very weak for six months. Now during this period she had no longer any obsessions. At the age of fifty-five she had a serious cerebral hemorrhage with hemiplegia of the right side and aphasia. Fortunately, after several months she recovered her speech and the movement of the right side in a quite remarkable way, and during the first minutes of a conversation with her one would not believe that she had had the hemorrhage. Yet there is a definite residual, and beyond any doubt Lise's psychological force has been greatly diminished. She has had to give up all the business matters to which she formerly gave her attention. She cannot follow a conversation or reading for more than a short time. She has become indifferent to the philosophical questions which formerly interested her. She remains in her easy chair for long periods without doing anything, which never happened before. But since her powers have been thus reduced this woman is no longer tormented by the obsessions which for years poisoned her existence.

These observations prove to us that obsessions do not depend solely on psychological depression and asthenia: a certain amount of agitation must be combined with this asthenia. Perhaps one might represent by a simple schema, such as that here given, this particular phase of depression which favors the development of obsession: One curve represents the oscillations in psychological activity, in psychological force. In the highest part of the curve, which corresponds to a state of normal excitation, obsession is not present. In the lowest part of the curve, in great depression, obsession is also absent. It is found only in a particular region of the curve, halfway up, when there is a slight depression mingled with agitation.

Patients with obsessions are at the same time both agitated and depressed, but their agitation is not of the passive sort which we have just associated with discharge; it is an active agitation of the same type as *effort*. Those with obsessions are sick people who suffer from their depression and their feelings of incompleteness, and they seek passionately for some stimulant which will get them

out of their depression. In 1912 I had occasion to present to the Academy of Moral Sciences a study of the mental state of the alcoholic, a study which I reproduced more completely in the third volume of my *Médications psychologiques* (pp. 173, 362). The alcoholic are not only sick after intoxication, but also before — before they have drunk anything. They are sick individuals, suffering from depression, incapable of leading a normal life, and they cannot tolerate their own impotence. They drink to stimulate themselves, to gain the feeling that they are living like others. Alcohol, like all psychic poisons, produces a mobilization of psychological forces which are called to the defense of the organism, and by this accumulation of forces it brings about a transitory elevation of the mind above its lower level. In all the compulsions, in the ruminations of the obsessed, there is a persistent recurrence of efforts, that is to say of clumsy efforts indefinitely repeated for the sake of stimulation of the same kind. This effort is not entirely absurd, because in serious circumstances courageous efforts have put an end to many depressions. How many depressed neurotics were cured during the war! But here the depression makes the efforts awkward and useless, and the patient is driven to begin them over and over again indefinitely.

The obsession becomes a first form of reaction against psychological asthenia by a reaction of effort, that is to say by increasing the action.[11] When this psychological weakness is a little more serious, or when it is found in individuals with a constitutional predisposition, it brings about another reaction, *fatigue*. We must not forget the fundamental distinction between exhaustion and fatigue: exhaustion is not a reaction, it is a particular condition of the organism and is characterized by a diminution of the available psychological forces. Fatigue and the feeling of fatigue, on the contrary, are reactions, special forms of conduct determined by this exhaustion at its beginning, and their purpose is to limit it, to hinder it from becoming complete and dangerous. The essence of this reaction is an active reduction of action, which is added to the preceding diminution due to weakness and often exaggerates it. It is manifested especially by different expressions of the feeling of fatigue and by the *devaluation of acts*. "Nothing has interest any longer, nothing is worth the least effort," and ever the characteristic expression of this condition: "*À quoi bon?* What's the use?" "I no longer want to do anything; I am waiting for the problem to solve itself; I am as if dead." It is always a question of the feeling of impotence, of the inaccessibility of all objectives, of the loss of confidence in oneself, of discouragement.

Certain forms of conduct become habitual and may be considered as symptoms; these are exaggerated reductions of action, precautions which patients take so as not to be drawn into action, which they wish to reduce as much as possible. One of these precautions is the habit of *lying*, which impresses me as very characteristic. If we wish to reduce action, it is important to reduce the social stimuli which would involve us in it. The mother demands that the child do its lessons, and if the child contrives to make his mother believe that the teacher has forgotten to assign work, the mother will stop demanding. Lying of this sort develops in children and young people who are asthenics, but it begins to disappear around the age of twenty, when social commands becomes less important; in the place of lying to other people the patient then develops the habit of lying to himself and finds refuge in the ideal and in dreaming.

Retrenchment (*le rétrécissement*) is another very important form of this diminution of action by the reaction of fatigue; it suppresses all that might be considered as only accessory to the action. Around any normal action there is a whole halo of little actions which serve to perfect the central one, finishing touches guided by feeling, which strictly speaking are not indispensable. The tired asthenic pays no attention to personal appearance, neglects social amenities, artistic labors, disinterested research. "What's the use?" Many neuropathic symptoms, especially in hysteria, are of this sort. Is it not true that some apparent anesthesias, such as unusual types of indifference, are really "scotomizations," as M. Pichon has said? Does not the patient conduct himself in the face of certain peripheral impressions in much the same way as we act in the face of a retinal scotoma which has ceased to attract our attention?

One may well ask if the well known *feelings of emptiness*, feelings of strangeness, of something never seen before, of something already seen, feelings of the artificial, the far-distant, the unreal, which play such an important part in so many neuroses, are not also the result of a kind of retrenchment. The subject who says: "It is no longer I who move, it is my hands. . . . I am a rubber ball rebounding of itself. . . . It is not my mother I see, but a good imitation of my mother," still has the essential perceptive faculties by which he recognizes the movement of his hands or the face of his mother, but he no longer adds the secondary feelings which characterize these perceptions as his own actions. He does not add to his actions the feeling of personal effort, or of maternal affection. The action is so much reduced, so retrenched, that it is no longer completely recognizable.

When psychological weakness and the reactions it determines become still more serious, we note the appearance of attacks of *anxiety* and of *escape from an action* to its exact opposite. The objects of the primary action are not merely deprived of meaning, artificial, or unreal; they become hateful, terrible, and dangerous. This characteristic is especially important in the case of social actions which have persons as their objects. The latter actions take on the most frightful aspects, and this dread of social action becomes the starting point for all the persecutory delusional states based on morbid interpretation. In another form social action becomes disintegrated: the subject can no longer distinguish what belongs to him from what belongs to other people, and he moves on toward the various forms of hallucinations of the paranoiac. The agitation and the discharges which are so important in asthenia give rise to reactions of triumph in other cases, and become the starting point of delusions of grandeur.

Thus all these secondary reactions determine a host of symptoms which are added to those resulting directly from the psychological asthenia, and this hypothesis of psychological weakness measured in terms of the characteristics of action permits the expression of a very large number of facts in the same type of language.

V. *Causes of Asthenia*

If we consider things from another point of view, the idea of psychological force and weakness can be applied not only to the symptoms of disease but also to the causes which bring them about. Psychological energy is manifested in the same way as electrical or chemical forces, of whose intimate nature we are ignorant but whose manifestations we can ascertain. The idea of this force is not something imaginary: it is the epitome of a whole group of objective observations of man's conduct, and it is quite possible to observe at the same time the material or social events which accompany and determine the modifications of these characteristics of conduct.

Our first and most important observation shows us that psychological force is a *hereditary* vital characteristic: we inherit psychological strength from our parents, just as we inherit their material fortunes. The most fortunate are perhaps those who have had healthy and unaffected parents who have not squandered this energy but have stored it up for their children. There are families of neurotics just as there are families of sound personality. In many families psychological weakness is apparent from childhood, and it plays a considerable part in what we call *constitution*. Several authors, as, for example, M. Henri Ey and M. Codet,[12] tell us that a constitution is the totality of the performed characteristics of the individual, which are present from the beginning of his biological existence and which are hereditary. These are complexes which signify permanent aptitudes, true psychic temperaments.

There is much talk today of *character* and of constitution. In my opinion there is not sufficient emphasis on the fact that the amount of psychological force which an individual possesses is just as much a fundamental trait of character as the amount of psychological tension. Most of the traits of character which are ordinarily cited depend strictly upon this psychological force: activity or laziness, habitual lying or truthfulness, sadness or gaiety, et cetera. There are characters which are predisposed from infancy to obsession and melancholy, "who in the face of the least difficulty give up the struggle and declare themselves vanquished." [13] Dispositions of this sort, which are reactions to certain forms of psychological asthenia, are just as constitutional and hereditary as the shape of one's nose or chin.

Great importance is assigned to the anatomical and histological study of the brain in various mental diseases, and it has yielded some interesting results even from the point of view of the psychologist. But here the difficulty which we pointed out at the very beginning of our study is most apparent: when it is a question of establishing some relationship between external phenomena, such as the appearance of the brain, and disorders of thought which seem to be characterized by a different type of knowledge — that of consciousness — and which are expressed in another language, that of psychology.

These difficulties disappear, or are diminished to a large extent, if one looks upon the idea of psychological force as an intermediary between phenomena of the mind and anatomical and physiological phenomena. Some interesting studies seem to show a relationship between psychological force and certain characteristics of the brain. I recall the interesting histological studies of M. Marchand, who observes that in many mental diseases, and particularly in some cases of that chronic and progressive asthenia which we call dementia praecox, many of the cells of the cortex are destroyed or altered. The psychological activity of the organism seems to him to be in relation to the number of cortical cells which are capable of functioning normally.

I also recall some experimental studies of the behavior of rats which had been deprived of a greater or less part of the cortex: the diminution of their ability to adapt themselves, their inability to find their way about in the maze as well as they did before the operation, seemed to depend not so much on the place of the lesion as on its extent.

In the clinic one observes this relationship between more or less extensive cerebral lesions and the symptoms of asthenia. I have often insisted on the results of the observation of a very interesting case, that of Captain Z— who was wounded in the occipital region during the war.[14] The first symptoms of cortical blindness, followed by hemianopsia, were at the beginning related to the site of the lesion; these symptoms were modified after several months, the visual affection took the form of concentric stricture, the form called hysterical, and to the end of his life the patient exhibited all the characteristics of severe psychological asthenia.

All cerebral diseases and all forms of encephalitis play a considerable part in the psychological asthenias. I have just mentioned the fact that one patient, Lise, who had been a severe obsessional case during her whole life, was completely cured as the result of a serious cerebral hemorrhage, which caused asthenia and suppressed her obsessional efforts. De Clérambault laid great emphasis on the importance of these traumata and infectious diseases which involve the brain. He made a splendid study of the difference in the results according to the age at which the brain is involved.[15] It seems to me he was less fortunate when he attempted to explain the appearance of the symptoms, especially of hallucinations, by a "serpiginous extension of the lesion," which gradually gained possession of certain cells. M. Ludo van Bogaert seems to me more exact when he states that following the lesion there is "a giving way of the affective unity of the individual" (it seems to me more exact to say a giving way of the psychological force), and that it is a psychological mechanism put into operation by this weakness which induces this or that symptom, in particular in M. van Bogaert's study, the objectification of the subject's ideas.[16] In this author's opinion certain symptoms, sleep for example, are, as we have just remarked, a direct manifestation of this giving way of the feeling self, a manifestation of the asthenia itself.

One must not forget that psychological asthenia is not only related to cerebral lesions and diseases, but that it appears after any sort of lesion or disease of the organism. I have seen serious cases of asthenia arise from extensive burns, abortions, surgical operations, hysterectomies, or removal of the gall bladder. We are familiar with many cases of psychological exhaustion, sometimes of long duration, as the result of typhoid fever or enteritis, although these diseases do not seem to have touched the brain. The study of these asthenias which follow illness will be very important. Today a new medical procedure (which seems to me by the way quite dangerous) treatment by hypoglycemia, and hypoglycemic coma caused by insulin, will perhaps allow us to study experimentally the development of these asthenias.

The distinction between asthenia properly so called and the various reactions which follow it — effort, laziness, anxiety, or the reaction of triumph — will perhaps permit us to give a more precise meaning to phrases which are very common but badly defined, the words "organic troubles" and "functional troubles." In reality all troubles are organic and imply an anatomical modification, either permanent or temporary, but some are more, some less, directly connected with a lesion and with asthenia. Some show a direct relationship and, unless there are substitutions, which are always possible, will probably last as long as the lesion; we call these organic. Others are reactions to this asthenia, and they may disappear when the organism becomes habituated to them and ceases to react to the original disturbance.[17] This distinction has some importance, even from the point of view of treatment: "To say that a disease is functional is to say that a modification of function can change it. On the other hand, to say that a disease is organic is to assert that the lesion and its direct manifestations will not be influenced by a modification of function."[18]

It is not only lesions of the organism which modify the psychological force. We can observe most interesting modifications in connection with the social milieu in which the individual moves. In the future, psychologists will be more interested than they are now in the milieu in which the patient lives, in the occupation he has followed for a long time, and even in his financial condition. One may mention the disorders of those individuals who have always lived healthy lives in the simple surroundings of the country, and who, when transferred to the city, are exhausted by a type of life which is too complicated for them. As Manouvrier has said, there is a special psychology of poverty, and a psychology of riches. We have already alluded to this fact in our discussion of timidity.

It is above all necessary to keep in mind the group which immediately surrounds the patient, the group of his intimate friends. Continual association with friends is sometimes a source of stimulation and enrichment, but it is very often a source of expenditure of energy and exhaustion. I have insisted elsewhere on the strange problem of the contagion of the neuroses. It will be said that as neuroses are not infectious diseases they cannot be really contagious,[19] yet I have investigated a phenomenon which seems to me very strange: I collected data on thirty households in which at the beginning one of the spouses was healthy and the other seriously neurotic, and I discovered that after ten years of living together both of the subjects were ill and depressed. In this case, contagion is a sort of exhaustion brought about by the continual presence of an individual who is tiring and exhausting, that is, "expensive."

This idea of expensive individuals, of individuals who are inexpensive, and of remunerative individuals, is essential for an understanding of the troubles of social groups and of households. A man wishes to get married and looks about for an energetic woman, capable of helping him to overcome his hesitations and doubts. He meets a young girl who attracts him because she seems decided, but he is mistaken; in reality she is as weak as he, and in spite of his age she too has been hoping to find some support in marrying him. The mistake brings about a serious depression in both and gives rise to a very strange hatred between them. This hatred is of interest to me in studying the origin of certain persecutory delusions.

We all need a certain stimulation which comes from our immediate environment. We have noticed this need in studying all sorts of social obsessions in the search for domination, for love, for flattery, et cetera. Our patients are only exaggerating a general tendency, because we all seek obedience, compliments, courtesies, which are the vitamins of the spirit. We give no thought to the importance of these polite acts, which we consider insignificant, because we have them in abundance. We are in the same situation as a man who has eaten well and cannot understand the fellow who wishes to steal a piece of bread. About us there are people whose lives are drab, who have no family, no friends, no pupils, no subordinates, and who never receive a compliment nor a polite gesture: "The sad thing about the little city in which I live," said one of these men, "is that I never have the opportunity to tip my hat. . . . If some day I should find a visiting card in my mailbox I would be transformed for a fortnight." One does not realize the great part which the presence or absence of exciting and stimulating people plays in our minds, but one must do it justice in the study of persecutory delusions.

There are many other difficulties which are worth consideration in the formation of groups; often the introduction of a new individual into a group gives rise to rivalries and jealousies, makes life more difficult, and brings on the exhaustion of some one of the members. There are badly formed groups which are too complex, and which have in their midst individuals whose character and psychological force vary too greatly; as M. Ch. Blondel has wittily said, "The man who is brought up to love the rhythm of slow waltzes is breathless with a partner who quivers at the sound of a jazz band. He declares that love is bankrupt, because for him his style of loving was love itself." [20] Repeatedly there occur false situations which require a more intelligent and more expensive adaptation, and which finally bring about exhaustion.

The study of the modifications of psychological force, again, affords room for interesting researches on the influence of past behavior on present psychological states. In my youth, after some very interesting observations, I came to assign some importance to an idea which is perhaps too philosophical, that the present behavior of a man depends on his past and on his more or less conscious memory of his own actions. The early observations which I published from 1886 to 1894 show that actual neuropathic accidents seem still to be determined by reactions to incidents in the past life that caused violent emotions, and that the more or less conscious memory of these events comes up again and modifies at least the form of present behavior. Certain observations which I published especially in 1889 and 1892 are quite characteristic.

At the time, I explained this form of neurosis — in my books and in the lectures which I gave at the Salpétrière in the clinic of Charcot — by saying that the efforts of the subject to react to a difficult and painful situation had not succeeded in completely liquidating the event by assimilating it to the history of the personality. The efforts had continued indefinitely because the problem was never solved, and the more or less conscious memory of the event brought about the exhaustion and the actual symptoms by this constantly repeated expenditure of energy; it was a question of *traumatic reminiscence.*

From these interpretations I drew an interesting conclusion from the therapeutic point of view. To put an end to this interminable and dangerous task it was beneficial to search carefully for such events with such memories in the past life of the patient, to recall them clearly to his consciousness, and to help the patient to carry out now, although somewhat late, the reaction necessary to bring about the psychological liquidation. At that time I published my observations, and in my courses I showed a rather large number of patients who had improved considerably through treatment of this kind.

However, after 1895 the number of these publications became less, and I appeared to have lost interest in these interpretations and treatments. This was not quite the truth, because in all my later works I recurred to the interest of these first studies, with the proviso, of course, that one should not generalize the conclusions to an exaggerated degree. This is especially apparent in the long chapter on therapeutic liquidation which is in the second volume of my *Médications psychologiques* (1919; pp. 204, 272).[21] Again recently, in an article in the *Annales medico-psychologiques* (October 1935), I insisted on a case which I find very interesting, in which the difficulty of liquidation brought on phenomena of non-realization and obsessions of realization, but it is true that I have appeared to assign less importance to these investigations of traumatic reminiscences. When I was working at the Salpétrière in the clinic of Charcot, of Brissaud, and of Raymond, I saw too many patients, too many cases of neurosis and psychosis, in whom traumatic reminiscences, although always sought for with great care, had evidently played an insignificant part. I therefore came to modify somewhat my first philosophical conception: the present behavior of a man and his present troubles do not depend solely upon his personal past and his own previous actions. The reminiscences are only a very small part of the influences which act on him. They are of interest only in special and fairly rare cases. One must also consider heredity, lesions of all sorts, present diseases and even past ones, the social milieu in which the patient has lived, and the countless influences which have made him what he is.

Is it not true that the original incident of the traumatic reminiscence was emotionally disturbing for the very reason that the subject was already in an abnormal condition because of other influences? Are we not taking a risk in fixing our attention and that of the patient on one small particular fact, while there were really a thousand others of the very same kind? Has not this event itself caused symptoms by other means than a more or less conscious memory? Ought we still today attempt to make the patient react to this past event as if it were present? Allow me to borrow a comparison from phenomena of another order. A young man of twenty contracted gonorrhea; and it was proper at that time to give him injections of permanganate. He returns when he is forty with a stricture of the posterior urethra. Must one treat him again with injections of permanganate, although the gonococcus no longer exists, and although it has left another lesion in its place? It is not by constantly calling up and discussing a past event that we suppress the anomalies and exhaustion which it has caused. The emotionally disturbing event and the prolonged absence of liquidation have transformed the mind and have left behind a new constitution, partly analogous to the first hereditary constitution. These are semi-constitutional troubles of a different kind from the doubt and hesitation at the moment of the past event. In the present symptoms of the patient there is undoubtedly something incidental in relation to present happenings, something constitutional which depends on heredity, and something semi-constitutional connected with the subject's past physical and personal life. In the light of the past event and of the troubles which it has caused there have occurred modifications of behavior, transformations of the psychological force (which has been diminished), an entirely different psychological equilibrium, in which the patient has settled. Calling up the memory of unsuccessful speculations of times gone by and constantly repeating the things he ought to have done will not prevent the loss of his fortune nor change his present poverty.

The emotion which diminished and disorganized the psychological forces has placed the patient in an entirely new situation, requiring the establishment of a completely new balance of forces, whatever the past circumstance may have been which caused this modification.[22] One must live in the present, and it is not always useful to begin the past all over again in order to live in the present.

Treatment by the liquidation of some traumatic reminiscences is still useful and serviceable in certain special cases, but unfortunately such cases are rare; and it is necessary before using this method to make a more exact diagnosis. One will have to make a diagnosis of those cases in which permanganate is still useful, and of those cases in which it will still be useful to make the patient relive the past event. The essential thing is always to understand the causes of the present asthenia, which may be numerous, and no philosophical theory will take the place of medical diagnostics. One can hope that the knowledge of these forms of psychological exhaustion and of the conditions in which psychological activity increases or diminishes will allow one to carry out with greater precision and success the treatment of many patients.

The treatment of the psychological asthenias, which are the starting point of many neuroses, should consist first of all in an economy of mental force, for in order to accumulate wealth one must first and above all reduce one's expenses. Many methods of rest, of isolation, and even of the liquidation of traumatic reminiscences, are basically only methods of economy. Psychotherapy must also attempt to make the patient acquire new habits and tendencies that will lessen the necessary efforts of adaptation. Perhaps, at least in certain cases, it may be possible to help the subject to gain new force by a kind of psychological excitation. These stimulations spread throughout the whole organism and cause the mobilization of forces and that *psychological irradiation* of which William James has spoken. Psychotherapy will gradually become more and more a good administration of the energies of the mind.

It seems to me interesting that this language and this

interpretation, which takes into account acquired asthenias as well as congenital ones, allows one to express clearly and to show the kinship between many affections which modify the activity of a living organism — those which depend upon brain lesions as well as those which depend upon general diseases, or which are the result of the behavior of the individual himself. These studies are anatomical and physiological as well as psychological. I was happy to see this opinion expressed very accurately in a recent article by MM. Henri Claude and Henri Ey on hallucinations: "This psychology does not exclude, but rather calls for a physiological explanation, a fact which seems too often to be ignored by those who treat this conception of psychogenesis with great disdain." [23] There is a remark of the same kind in the interesting communication of M. Lacan on the paranoiac with their delusions.[24] Later, if this view develops a greater precision, it will be able to offer opportunity for measurements of tension and of psychological force, and will be instrumental in introducing comparisons and measurements into psychiatry.

In the description of the neuroses and the psychoses those observers who talk of consciousness and those who talk of cortical alterations are too far apart from one another. Besides, the diseases which they have established are foreign to each other, for they describe in comparative isolation an attack of nerves, an obsession, a delusion of grandeur. One may hope that the language of psychological strength and weakness will allow the various observers to describe the facts in the same tongue, and will make possible mutual criticism and understanding. The various diseases will no longer be so entirely foreign to each other, if they are presented as different instances of the balance between psychological receipts and expenditures.

That is why I dare to hope that this summary of long studies which began nearly forty years ago at this very place in my first lectures in the Harvard Medical School, and which are again presented at Harvard's Tercentenary, will be useful in the development of further investigations.

REFERENCES

1. Alfred Feuillée, in *Revue philosophique*, 1882, II, 617.
2. Pierre Janet, *De l'angoisse à l'extase* (Paris, 1926), II, 62, 121, 588, 606.
3. Pierre Janet, *Les obsessions et la psychasthénie* (Paris, 1903).
4. Pierre Janet, *La force et la faiblesse psychologiques* (Maloine, Paris, 1932).
5. Cf. Pierre Janet, *Les débuts de l'intelligence* (E. Flammarion, Paris, 1935) and *L'intelligence avant le langage* (E. Flammarion, Paris, 1936).
6. Théodule Ribot, "Le moindre effort en psychologie," *Revue philosophique*, 1910, II, 376.
7. Ch. Féré, "Dégénérescence et criminalité," *Revue philosophique*, 1887, II, 356.
8. Janet, *Les obsessions et la psychasthénie*, I, 559; *British Journal of Psychology: Medical Section*, October 1920; Pierre Janet, *Les médications psychologiques* (Alcan, Paris, 1919), II, 78, 79, 302 *et seq.*
9. Janet, *La force et la faiblesse psychologiques*, p. 276.
10. See note 3.
11. Janet, *De l'angoisse à l'extase*, II, 146, 198; *La force et la faiblesse psychologiques*, p. 135.
12. Henri Ey, "Les constitutions," *L'évolution psychiatrique*, 1932, p. 2; Codet, "Constitutions, mentalité, tempérament psychique," *ibid.*, p. 21; cf. Henri Wallon, "Syndromes d'insuffisance psycho-motrice et types psychomoteurs," *Annales médico-psychologiques*, April 1932, p. 374.
13. Janet, *De l'angoisse à l'extase*, II, 378, and *L'évolution psychologique de la personnalité* (Chahine, Paris, 1929).
14. Janet, *De l'angoisse à l'extase*, II, 68, 110, 218; *La force et la faiblesse psychologiques*, p. 279.
15. De Clérambault, "Psychoses à base d'automatisme," *Pratique médicale française*, May 1925, p. 189.
16. Ludo van Bogaert (d'Anvers), "L'hallucinose pédonculaire," *Revue neurologique*, May 1927, p. 613.
17. Pierre Janet, *Les névroses* (Paris, 1909), p. 373; *De l'angoisse à l'extase*, II, 658.
18. Janet, *Les médications psychologiques*, II, 234.
19. Janet, *Les médications psychlogioques*, II, 183.

20. Charles Blondel, *Introduction à la psychologie collective* (A. Colin, Paris, 1928), p. 166.

21. Cf. Janet, *De l'angoisse à l'extase*, II, 352; *La force et la faiblesse psychologiques*, p. 221.

22. Cf. Janet, *De l'angoisse à l'extase*, II, 488.

23. *Annales médico-psychologiques*, October 1932, pp. 273–316.

24. Jacques Lacan, *De la psychose paranoïaque dans ses rapports avec la personnalité* (E. Le François, Paris, 1932), p. 129.

LOGIC

RUDOLF CARNAP, DR.PHIL., S.D.

*Professor of Philosophy, University of Chicago (formerly of the
Deutsche Universität, Prague)*

WHEN we reflect upon the behavior of men, whether
of individuals or of groups, we see that they are
dominated more by their passions than by their reason.
Especially when surveying contemporary society, one
could almost despair of the role of logic as a factor determining human behavior. Nevertheless, to see clearly on
the matter, it is essential that we obtain an adequate conception of the province of logic. By doing so we will be able
to distinguish between thinking which is irrational or
illogical and thinking which is reasonable or logical, and
thus win a richer understanding of the ways in which
logical and illogical thought may influence the activities of
men.

The cardinal point about which we must become clear is
that logic is not concerned with human behavior in the
same sense that physiology, psychology, and social sciences are concerned with it. These sciences formulate
laws or universal statements which have as their subject
matter human activities as processes in time. Logic, on
the contrary, is concerned with *relations* between factual
sentences (or thoughts). If logic ever discusses the truth
of factual sentences it does so only *conditionally*, somewhat as follows: *if* such-and-such a sentence is true, *then*
such-and-such another sentence is true. Logic itself does
not decide whether the first sentence *is* true, but sur-

renders that question to one or the other of the empirical sciences. Consequently, since the rules of logic refer simply to various *relations* between sentences (or thoughts), we can distinguish between thinking which is in accordance with these rules and thinking which violates them. The former we shall call *logical thinking*, the latter *illogical*. On the other hand, although logic itself is not concerned with facts, a process of thought, whether it be logical or illogical, is an actual fact. And it is a question of greatest importance, both for the individual and for society, whether our thinking is logical or not.

Contemporary logical theory is too vast and technical to be summarized here. It is, however, possible to view at least a part of this theory as defining the conditions of logical thought. And in what follows, I wish to consider the requirements which thinking must satisfy in order to be logical or reasonable. These requirements can be summarized briefly under the following three heads: clarity, consistency, and adequacy of evidence.

1. The *condition of clarity* may be formulated as follows. We must become clear as to what is the subject of our talking and thinking. Although this requirement may seem trivial, in practice it is often not observed. The most serious and frequent breaches of this rule occur whenever sentences are uttered which are taken to assert something, although in fact nothing is asserted, whether truly or falsely. Such self-deceptions have their source, for the most part, in the structure of our common-day language. For our common language is well adapted for obtaining the gross agreements necessary in practical affairs; but when employed in theoretical pursuits to formulate and communicate knowledge, it is very often not merely inadequate but even seriously misleading.

A little reflection will therefore show that we must distinguish between two main functions which expressions may have. Certain expressions in our language assert something, and are therefore either true or false. Such expressions exercise a *cognitive function* and have a cognitive meaning. On the other hand, certain expressions express the emotions, fancies, images, or wishes of the speaker, and under proper conditions evoke emotions, wishes, or resolutions in the hearer. Such expressions will be said to exercise an *expressive function*, and it is possible to subdivide them further into expressions with pictorial, emotional, and volitional functions. An expression may exercise these different expressive functions simultaneously; and it often is the case that a sentence with cognitive meaning may also possess one or more of the expressive functions. It is of prime importance to note that not all expressions of our language possess a cognitive meaning, so that we must distinguish between those which do and those whose function is solely expressive.

This distinction is frequently concealed by the fact that sentences with solely expressive functions sometimes have the grammatical form of statements which are either true or false. Hence we are led to believe, quite mistakenly, that such sentences do have cognitive meaning. When a lyric poet sings of the melancholy forest or the friendly gleam of moonlight, his utterances take the form of factual statements. However, everyone realizes that the poem is not to be taken as a factual description of the forest or the moon; for it is tacitly understood that the lyric poem is simply expressive of a mood, exactly as music is. But what is so evident in poetry is often far from clear in philosophy. Careful logical analysis has shown that many sentences uttered by trans-empirical metaphysicians appear to have cognitive meaning simply because their grammatical form is that of genuine assertions, although in fact these utterances exercise a solely expressive function. For example, a metaphysician may say, "The fact that all objects in nature, down to the smallest particles of matter, attract and repel one another, is to be explained by the love and hate which these objects bear toward one another." If such a metaphysician supposes that his explanation adds anything to our knowledge of the empirical facts of attraction and repulsion, he is grossly in error, misled by his language. For his statement (or better, pseudo-statement) asserts nothing whatsoever, and simply associates certain images and sentiments with our knowledge of the attraction and repulsion of bodies. His statement has, therefore, no cognitive meaning, although it has a pictorial and emotional function. It is neither true nor false, and belongs to poetry, not to science. Without question, many metaphysical utterances of this type influence our lives by stimulating our emotions and springs of action. Nevertheless, when such utterances are taken to be assertions and arguments are offered for them either *pro* or *con*, the partners to the controversy are deceiving themselves.

Unfortunately, this type of illogical thinking occurs also in fields other than philosophy. Philosophers constitute only a small proportion of mankind; and their doctrines and the confusions arising from their failure to distinguish between the cognitive and expressive function of sentences produce relatively little harmful effects upon human destiny. In any case, their influence is considerably less than is often alleged by many philosophers and philosophical historians. The consequences of the indicated confusion are much more serious when it occurs in discussions concerning individual or political conduct. When I say to some one "Come here!" it is evident that my words exercise a volitional function, and express my desire in order to evoke a certain response in my hearer. My utterance is not an assertion, and any debate about its truth or falsity would clearly be irrelevant. If a theoretical discussion were to arise concerning it, the debate would be significant only if it were to deal with such questions as whether the person addressed will obey me or what the consequences of his decision will be.

But although the matter is obvious for this simple case, the situation is not so readily apprehended when sentences expressing a command have the grammatical form of assertions. Frequent illustrations of this are found in politics, with serious practical consequences. For example, suppose that the following creed is promulgated in a certain country: "There is only one race of superior men, say the race of Hottentots, and this race alone is worthy of ruling other races. Members of these other races are inferior, so that all civil rights are to be denied them so long as they inhabit the country." This pronouncement certainly has the appearance of an assertion. Some of those who dissent from it, taking the grammatical form at face value, may regard it as a genuine assertion and may therefore propound a doctrine in opposition to it. In fact, however, the pronouncement has no cognitive meaning and exercises merely a volitional function. The true nature of the doctrine (or better, pseudo-doctrine) is made clear if we state the pronouncement in the imperative form, to reveal its exclusively volitional function. It then reads as follows: "Members of the race of Hottentots! Unite and battle to dominate the other races! And you, members of other races! Submit to the yoke or fly from this land!" It is now obvious that the political creed is a command, concerning which it is not significant to raise questions of truth or falsity. It is, of course, true that it is possible to raise cognitively significant issues in connection with such a command. But these will involve questions such as whether and to what degree the command will be executed, and what the consequences will be of obeying it or not. It is also possible to debate the factual statements about races, which are usually connected with the command; these are clearly scientific issues belonging to anthropology, and must be critically investigated by specialists in this field. It is, however, of great practical importance for understanding the effective appeal of political war-cries like the above to note that they take the form of misleading pseudo-assertions. This is to be explained by the fact that many men respond less readily to what are obviously commands than to such assertions or pseudo-assertions, especially when the latter are accompanied by powerful emotional appeals.

2. The *condition of consistency*, that our ideas agree with one another, is the second requirement for logical thinking. Logic is not competent to decide whether a judgment of ours having factual content is either true or false. However, logic is competent to determine whether our assertions or suppositions are consistent with one another. The task of logic may also be viewed as making evident the consequences of a given assumption, irrespective of its truth or falsity. For logic as the study of valid consequences is identical with logic as the inquiry into conditions of consistency, and the insight that one sentence follows from another is the same as the insight that the contradictory of the first is incompatible with the other. If, for example, I assume that iron does not float on water and that my latch-key is made of iron, the supposition that my latch-key will float on water is incompatible with my original assumptions. In order to avoid contradicting my own premises, I must therefore assume that my key will sink. Logic itself does not affirm this last assumption;

it simply renders explicit what is implicitly contained in the two premises previously assumed.

It will be clear, therefore, that the requirements of logic are much weaker than those of the empirical sciences. The latter demand of us that we accept certain assertions and reject others. Logic, however, does not prescribe what factual assertions we are to accept or reject; it simply demands that we do not at the same time accept and also reject an assertion. This demand is made in our own name, so to speak, by recalling to us our own intent and pointing out that to accept a given assertion would contravene some resolutions previously made.

This task of logic here indicated is far from being as trivial as it may appear at first glance. During the past one hundred years what is known as symbolic logic has been developed by Boole, Peirce, Frege, Whitehead, Russell, and many others. A vast treasure of validating forms, conditioning valid inferences, but unknown to traditional logic, has thus been discovered. It will here suffice to mention as an example the theory of relations worked out in detail by Peirce. The precise study of structures and order-types exemplified in different subject matters has become possible only on the basis of this theory. For example, geometry as the theory of a certain type of order applicable to space is simply a special instance of the general theory of relations. Moreover, one of the triumphs of modern logical research has been to demonstrate the fact that all of mathematics has the same status as logic itself. That is to say, mathematics has been shown to make no factual assertions of any kind, and is revealed as the instrument for exhibiting the relations of consistency and deducibility between assumptions concerning any subject matter whatsoever.

Philosophers have sometimes maintained that mathematics differs from the natural sciences in that the latter take actually existing objects as their subject matter, while the former studies ideal objects. The truth is, however, that mathematics no more than logic is concerned with any type of objects. Both mathematics and logic simply teach how we may make explicit the conclusions implicitly contained in given assumptions so that both are concerned with possible linguistic or conceptual forms, and not with objects of any description. In particular, what are usually designated in our disastrously misleading language by the substantive "numbers," are not entities of any sort; they are conceptual forms, forms of thought and statement, applicable to any empirical subject matter. The same conclusion is reached for mathematical functions, and even more obviously for the aggregates, groups, and fields of the more abstract branches of modern mathematics.

These points may become clearer in the context of a more concrete illustration. In order to build a bridge, the engineer must take into account certain laws of nature, partly formulated as general laws of mechanics and partly as specific laws of the materials to be employed. With the help of these laws he can calculate that a bridge with a specified structure is capable of carrying such-and-such a load. Now these laws are supplied to the engineer by the empirical sciences, in particular by physics. Mathematics and logic, on the other hand, enable him to deduce the strength of the bridge from the physical laws and the initial data concerning the details of its structure. The logico-mathematical instrument is thus essential for every type of rational, planned activity. This is true not only in constructing machines but also in organizing human associations and activities, for instance, in the field of economics for planning both individual enterprises and large-scale social undertakings. Without this instrument, it is clear that civilization as we know it today would not be possible.

3. *Adequacy of evidence* is the third requirement for logical thinking; this is the condition that there be a sufficiently secure empirical foundation both for the universal laws we formulate and for the predictions we make with their aid. The point of this requirement will be clear from the following illustration. The prediction is made that three years hence at 3 P.M. there will be a heavy rainfall at Cambridge. This assertion is unexceptionable with respect to its form. It is also consistent with the rest of our knowledge, since it contradicts no known facts or recognized laws. Nevertheless, the prediction violates the third kind of logical rules, namely, the methodological rules for factual thinking. The fundamental rule of scientific method requires that every assertion about anything not observed (for instance future events) must be securely connected with our knowledge concerning facts already observed. And it will be clear that this is not the case for the above prediction. However, in the present case, just as in matters of consistency, logic has only conditional judgments to offer: *if* such-and-such observation sentences are given, *then* a law of a specified kind has an adequate (or inadequate) empirical foundation. Such judgments constitute the *logic of empirical confirmation*. This branch of logic asserts, for example, that a law (that is, a universal sentence) is confirmed to a higher degree, the greater is the number of its instances which are confirmed by observation, provided that none of its instances are in disagreement with observation.

The progress that has been made in the theory of scientific method is due not only to professional philosophers, but even to a greater degree to natural scientists themselves.

Some of the eminent workers in this branch of logic have been Ernst Mach, Poincaré, Duhem, Peirce, and Russell, and in recent years modern symbolic methods have made it possible to formulate their results more exactly and to extend them. The interest in methodological problems is increasing; and I think that it is one of the hopeful signs of the times that various groups, in America as well as Europe, which concern themselves with these issues, are beginning to co-operate actively with one another.

It is not surprising that consequences disastrous for human behavior frequently follow, when, in situations of practical importance, the requirement of an adequate empirical basis for factual thinking is violated. Far-reaching conclusions concerning the conduct of a whole people are sometimes asserted on the basis of relatively meager and inadequate data obtained in psychological laboratories. For example, the statistics of intelligence tests upon men drafted for army service have been used to bolster up the view that most men are slaves by nature, and to support the prediction that the run of mankind is incapable of higher forms of civilization. Indeed, it is not necessary to press the point that in daily life this important third condition for logical thinking is fulfilled more often in the breach than in observance. Men expect a future which will satisfy their hopes and desires, even when such expectations are inadequately based on observed facts. A naïve chess-player expects that his opponent will make just those moves which will fall in with his own plan; he does not stop to think that it would be more reasonable to await a move which could favor his opponent's game. In the same way, deceived by their desires, men count on just that behavior in others which would coincide with their own needs. It is in this way that we must explain the conduct of different nations, races, and social classes, since, unfortunately, their conduct is controlled more often by passions than by reflection upon the facts of psychology and the social sciences. Their expectations, inadequately founded, are usually followed by disappointments in the behavior of other parties; but the failures of their hopes, instead of leading to the correction of erroneous assumptions, frequently become the occasions for a childish reproval of opposing groups in the name of morality.

The conditions which logic sets for rational thinking and which we have now surveyed, are not to be understood as possessing some absolute metaphysical validity or as resting on the will of God. The requirements made by logic are based on the simple fact that unless they are satisfied, thought and knowledge cannot perform their function as instruments for arriving at successful decisions in practical matters. Now since our actual thinking frequently violates the requirements of logic, it follows that illogical thought is an important factor in determining human behavior. Indeed, certain anti-rationalistic tendencies of our day preach the view that reason should be esteemed less, and that men ought to assign a smaller role to rational thought in practical life. Furthermore, the confusions in practice and doctrine which are to be found in society, science, and art are asserted to be consequences of overvaluating the intellect. In fact, however, it is not of much importance whether men think much or little; it is of far greater consequence, *if* they think at all, whether their thinking is logical or not. And advocates of irrationalism are most successful in strengthening men in their biases and prejudices, confirming mankind in its errors instead of disciplining men's thoughts to aim at objectivity.

Logic must often play the role of the critic, especially in our own day. Its task is to serve as a spiritual hygiene, cautioning men against the disease of intellectual confusion. It has the ungrateful duty, whenever it finds symptoms of this disease, to pronounce the unwelcome diagnosis. But in what manner, it may be asked, shall we conduct the therapeutic treatment? The logician by himself has no remedy to offer, and must turn to psychologists and social scientists for aid; for it is obvious that the mere discovery and acknowledgment of errors have no significant influence upon the thoughts and actions of men. Logic can point out the anomalies, but it is psychology which must find curative methods for them.

Logicians sometimes imagine that they can effect practical changes by their critical analyses. Such an expectation, however, itself violates the requirement of adequate empirical foundation. It is based simply on our desires, in utter disregard of facts clear to every observer of individual and social behavior. The laws of human conduct in observing and violating the requirements of logical thinking must be discovered by psychology and the social sciences. These are the disciplines which must locate the irrational sources of both rational and illogical thought. This theoretical problem once solved, it then becomes the practical task of education, conceived in the broadest sense, to apply suitable methods for healing the indicated anomalous behavior. Indeed, a far better aim of education and a more effective program for it is the establishment of prophylactic methods for eliminating the source of illogical types of thought. Logic itself, however, must remain content with the more modest task of pointing them out.

AN EXAMPLE FROM THE EVIDENCE
OF HISTORY

Abbott Lawrence Lowell, LL.D., Litt.D., L.H.D.

President, Emeritus, of Harvard University

WHEN asked to illustrate from political history the principles brought out in this symposium on "Factors Determining Human Behavior," I felt that whoever might be learned and discerning enough to do so, it was wholly impossible for me. The utmost I could do would be to take some specific method of attaining a political result and describe a particular case of its use; and in doing so I am stating nothing that is not perfectly well known.

Anyone who observes the habits of animals and birds can hardly fail to be impressed by how well, in most cases, they are fitted to attain the three main objects of their lives — getting food, not being food for others, and rearing their young. Nor is this, like the case of those insects whose habits have remained the same from geologic ages, the result of an instinct fully developed with the creature; for their behavior sometimes changes greatly if the conditions in which they live are altered — as, for example, when the rats in Jamaica became arboreal after the introduction of the mongoose. Ordinarily, the habitat and the physical powers of their wild enemies, and hence their own danger, change little, so that they have not much adjustment to make; but when man comes on the scene it is different, and yet they learn with no little rapidity the increasing range of his firearms, and the protection to be found in his sanctuaries.

All this is so true that naturalists tell us they would rarely find it possible, if consulted by their wild friends, to give them advice about improving their mode of life in these respects. They admit that they could not by logical thought suggest a better code of conduct than these creatures have worked out for their own guidance. And yet we do not suppose that such habits have been formed on any consistent and comprehensive plan. They have been the result of adapting their action to meet this, that, and the other difficulty as it arose; and when the environment has been such that their various needs could be met by lines of conduct not seriously interfering with one another, there has developed a consistent and harmonious pattern of behavior. If not, such a pattern could not be formed, and the creature would have had to find some other habitat or disappear altogether. Of course those that have survived are the ones that have found such an adjustment possible.

This does not mean that the system of life so evolved is perfect for each of the objects to be attained, but that it is good enough for all of them to produce a self-consistent whole; and the method of its formation is virtually that of trial and error. A naturalist with whom I was conversing on this subject some time ago agreed that most of the higher animals could in this way work out patterns of behavior well adapted to their needs, and had done so; but he added that man could not. Is the last statement always true, or do men, by conscious and intentional attempts to attain immediate ends, sometimes develop a harmonious system which they neither desired nor foresaw? In asking this question we must bear in mind that with animals persistent courses of action produce habits, with men they produce institutions and all the associated ideas (called by Pareto "derivations") that gather about them. The institution that I shall use as an illustration is that of the

British parliamentary system, whereby the House of Commons is controlled by the ministry of the day, itself composed of the leaders of a party organization entrusted with power as the result of a general election. Anyone who has tried to teach the actual working of modern governments will have recognized that of England as the easiest to explain because it is rational. Mark, I am speaking of function not structure. The structure, that is the legal form of the English government, is highly complex, and there seems to be no desire among statesmen to make it less so. When the Board of Education was established, nearly forty years ago, it was criticized on the ground that a single executive head would be more in accord with present practice; but the Duke of Devonshire, with that transparent frankness that caused him to yawn in the middle of his own speeches, remarked that although the point was mooted when the bill was first prepared, he quite admitted that he was unable to recollect the reasons which weighed in favor of a Board rather than a secretary of state, but added that it was perfectly well understood there would be no real Board at all.

I propose to show that the parliamentary system as it now stands was by no means contemplated by the men who brought it about; that it was in fact quite contrary to their theories of government; that the steps they took were consciously and rationally taken to meet certain immediate needs without a thought of possible ultimate consequences; but that they naturally led to the system finally evolved.

Let us recall the framework of the English political system at the beginning of the eighteenth century. For our present purpose a very general statement will suffice, since only with the large outlines shall we deal. After the long struggle for power in the preceding century — running through the execution of the King and the abolition of the monarchy, the revulsion that followed, and the attempt of James II to increase the royal power which ended in his flight and the Revolution of 1688 — after all these events the legal situation became singularly stable. The independence of the courts, their authority to decide what the law is and how it shall be applied in particular cases, was implicit in the Revolution and completed by the Act of Settlement; nor did it change during the whole evolution of the parliamentary system. In fact, as Freeman pointed out, the subsequent growth of the conventions on which that system rests could not have taken place until the supremacy of the law had been firmly established.

The new monarchy enjoyed prerogatives, not, indeed, so great as those claimed by James II, and not exactly defined in every detail, but still fairly precise in their general scope. They included the central administration, with the selection and direction of the agents by which the government was to be carried on; and from a purely legal point of view these prerogatives have remained substantially unchanged to the present day. The legislative power was vested in Parliament, composed of king, lords and commons; and, save for a shearing of the power of the House of Lords in the present century, this also has remained legally unchanged ever since. The essential progress has been in the methods of exercising these permanent legal powers whereby the whole nature of the system has in fact been radically transformed. Let us look at the process by which this has been brought to pass.

By 1702 the childless king had evidently a short time to live, and the one remaining successor provided by the revolutionary act was an elderly widow whose last child had died the year before. Obviously some new provision must be made for filling the throne, and this was done in favor of the Hanoverian family by the Act of Settlement of that year. In the Act various provisions were inserted for the conduct of public affairs under the new sovereigns; one of them, designed to prevent the monarch from obtaining an undue influence over the House of Commons, forbade any-one holding an office of place or profit under the crown from having a seat there. It was clearly based on the prin-ciple of the separation of powers; as was also a standing order of the House, adopted about the same time, that proposals for expenditure should be received only on the recommendation of the crown. This last, although by no means so intended, later proved important in securing the control of the cabinet over Parliament, and has remained to the present day. But the provision excluding the minis-ters of state from sitting in the Commons after the death of Queen Anne was seen to involve a practical difficulty be-cause the appropriations they needed and the measures they desired had to be explained to the members, and the easiest way of doing so was to follow the practice that had grown up of speaking from their seats in the House. There-fore the Act of Settlement was amended in the early years of Queen Anne's reign to permit them to be elected and sit there. Clearly this was not done with any idea that it would change the generally accepted principle of the sepa-ration of powers, but as an immediate convenience — a case of meeting a present difficulty by an action purposely taken to overcome it, and no more.

At that period the crown, in theory and largely in prac-tice, selected its ministers, like all its other servants, as it pleased; but, since the assent of Parliament for appropria-tions and legislation was essential, it became more and more needful that the ministers should be able to obtain that assent, and therefore to lead a majority in the House. Hence men with divergent political views and ambitions

strove to acquire or retain the great offices of state by being
the leaders in Parliament — in short by controlling the
House of Commons, which began to be a battlefield for and
against the ministers. This developed into a recognized
practice during the long administration of Sir Robert Walpole. Not that continuous political parties in office and
opposition were yet developed. That came later. But there
were groups and factions fighting for power, with their constant struggles in the House. So action and reaction were
equal and opposite; the House acquiring a decisive influence over the composition of cabinets and the ministers
striving to gain power over its members. All of which was
done, not with any conscious design of changing the
method of government, but in each case with a view — a
distinct, intelligent purpose — of accomplishing an immediate object; and the process went on until very gradually the present system was evolved.

That system is singularly self-consistent and harmonious
in its operation, more so than any other now existing or
perhaps that ever did exist. Whether it will tend in the
long run to the greatest welfare of the British people is a
different question with which we are not here concerned;
but it works smoothly. Through an alternation in power
of the competing parties, determined by the majority in
the House of Commons — which when formed is in turn
directed by the body of party leaders in the cabinet — it
gives effect to the popular will with great speed and very
little friction; with much talk no doubt, but practically
no violence. Whether statesmen could have excogitated
such a system in advance, how nearly they would have hit
upon it if they had tried, and how well they would have
been pleased with it when found, are interesting questions.
But, in fact, the present parliamentary system was not in
accord with the preconceived ideas of Englishmen at the

time it was being evolved, and even when it was well on its way towards its final goal. That it was, indeed, quite inconsistent with their theories on the subject, and destined to reverse them, must now be shown.

The disturbances of the seventeenth century gave rise in England to many treatises on government, some of them describing imaginary communities, others discussing the basic conditions of political society, but all dealing essentially with the source of power rather than the relation to each other of constituted authorities. For our purpose they throw no significant light on the origins of the parliamentary system. The latest, and the one that has had the greatest influence, was published after the Revolution of 1688 by John Locke in his *Two Treatises of Government*; but these also have a general character, and although he assumes the separation of legislative and executive power (opening of Book II, chap. XII), he does not discuss the matter, or explain why it is important and how it is to be carried out.

In the eighteenth century, however, there were three systematic portrayals of the actual, or what was supposed to be the actual, system of government in England, by a Frenchman, a Swiss, and an Englishman; the two foreigners having lived in England, and the third being a barrister, professor, member of Parliament, and justice of the Court of Common Pleas—singularly well qualified, therefore, to know both the theory and practical working of the British constitution.

The first of these is by the Baron de Montesquieu, whose celebrated *Esprit des Lois* appeared in 1748, after the struggle of ministers and prospective ministers to retain or acquire control of the House of Commons was well developed. He had spent two years in England during Walpole's administration, was a friend of Lord Chesterfield, and should have been familiar with the existing conditions in English public life. Chesterfield, indeed, in his letters to his son, shows that he understood perfectly well the actual relation of ministers to the management of the House and the election of its members (Letters CCLXVIII and CCLXXVI). The *Esprit des Lois* is a curious mixture of fact and fancy, of description and theory, and the examples he gives seem rather illustrations of his principles than the ground of their formation.

The important chapter for our purpose is that entitled "De la constitution d'Angleterre," and although the account contained therein takes the form of what the institutions of a state should be in order to maintain the liberty of the citizen, it is obvious that he meant to describe those of England. Here it is that he sets forth the doctrine of the separation of the executive, legislative, and judicial powers as essential, showing no suspicion of the growing connection of the first two through the position of the ministers in parliament. The chapter ends, indeed, with the remark: "It is not for me to examine whether the English actually enjoy this liberty or not; for me it is enough that it is established by their laws, and I look no farther." It would be more accurate to say that the laws, written and traditional, establish the separate existence of the crown and the houses, but neither provide that in actual operation they shall not be under a common control, nor place any impediments in the way of their being so.

For a time the *Esprit des Lois* was not well received in France, but people in England were enthusiastic about it, and especially about the remarks on their government. They do not seem to have recognized that Montesquieu's description of the British system was no longer true of the actual conditions, or that his basic theory of the separation of the legislative and executive functions was in practice being outgrown; for they still clung to the conceptions of the glorious Revolution of 1688.

Not less notable, though perhaps less surprising, was the success of the Swiss DeLolme's book on the English Constitution, which was published in Amsterdam in 1771, with an English edition in the following year. It is essentially a eulogy of the British government on the conventional lines; for he writes (chap. x) of the promotion of liberty by the separation of the legislative and executive authority, and treats as one of the excellencies of the system (chap. IV) the fact that the laws are initiated, not by the crown or ministers, but by the members of Parliament —a condition that in his sense had long ceased to be true. Obviously he had no more idea than Montesquieu of the change taking place in the relations between the ministers and the Commons, although it had progressed farther in the fourteen years between the publication of their books. DeLolme goes on to remark (Book II, chap. XVII, p. 375) that English liberty is due to the impossibility of the leaders in Parliament "invading and transferring to themselves any branch of the executive authority" — although the question which of them should succeed in doing that very thing was what the leaders were all the time fighting about. Finally he tells us (pp. 477–78) that the English government will be no more, either when the crown shall become independent of the nation for its supplies, or when the representatives of the people begin to share in the executive authority. The first of these has not happened; the second, at the very time he wrote, was, through the connection with the ministers, proceeding constantly.

Men prominent in English public life spoke highly of this work, although, had they thought about the matter, they could hardly have failed to perceive that one of the cardinal points of DeLolme's whole theory, the sharp

separation of the executive and legislative powers, had
long ceased to exist. But conceptions outlast the foundations on which they are built, and statesmen unused to
analytic thought beyond their own province may well
repeat, and suppose that they believe, a statement clearly
no longer true, as may be seen from the third, and in this
respect the most strange, of the writings to be cited.

Sir William Blackstone, then a barrister and afterwards a
judge, lectured at Oxford on the Common Law, and in 1765
published his *Commentaries on the Laws of England*. It
was a masterly production which has been read more
widely and longer than any other legal work in countries
where the Common Law prevails. In this great book he
included the laws relating not only to civil rights but also
to the public authorities; and if he had confined himself
strictly to the law his statements would have been perfectly correct; for, as we have seen, the legal powers of the
organs of the British government have changed very little
since the revolutionary settlement. But Blackstone strove
both to expound the laws of England and to justify them,
to point out their excellence, their almost complete perfection. The whole work concludes, indeed, with the naïve
remark: "We have taken occasion to admire, at every
turn, the noble monument of ancient simplicity, and the
more curious refinements of modern art. Nor have its
faults been concealed from view; for faults it has, lest we
should be tempted to think it of more than human structure."

In this spirit he describes the distribution of power
among the public authorities, and says (Book I, chap. II):
"In all tyrannical governments, the supreme magistracy,
or the right of *making*, and of *enforcing* the laws, is vested
in one and the same man, or one and the same body of
men; and wherever these two powers are united together,

there can be no public liberty. . . . With us, therefore, in England, this supreme power is divided into two branches; the one legislative, to wit, the parliament, consisting of king, lords and commons; the other executive, consisting of the king alone." He goes on (a few pages later) to explain why the crown should have a power of rejecting, but only of rejecting, a statute — a power, by the way, which had become obsolete at the death of Queen Anne — for otherwise there would be a tendency to tyranny; and he proceeds: "And herein indeed consists the true excellence of the English government, that all the parts of it form a mutual check upon each other. . . . Thus every branch of our civil polity supports and is supported, regulates and is regulated by the rest: for the two houses naturally drawing in two directions of opposite interest, and the prerogative in another still different from them both, they mutually keep each other from exceeding their proper limits; while the whole is prevented from separation, and artificially connected together by the mixed nature of the crown, which is a part of the legislature, and the sole executive magistrate."

In short, he accepted the current political philosophy of the day based upon conditions that had ceased to exist, and his contemporaries — even those in active political life — did the same. The men who guided the affairs of state worked out, by continual adaptation of actions to particular definite objects, a harmonious system the real nature of which few people understood until Bagehot explained it to them in the seventh decade of the nineteenth century. It may be stated of the makers of the British parliamentary government as has been said of Columbus, that when he started on his voyage he did not know where he was going, when he got there he did not know where he was, and when he got back he did not know where he had been; and yet he discovered America. Like his the action was intentional, and in its direct objects perfectly logical, but led naturally to results wholly unexpected. I think, therefore, the example of the British parliamentary system shows that with men, as with animals, a continual conscious adaptation to immediate objects may sometimes, if the conditions are favorable, lead to a fully self-consistent and harmonious system which to the authors is quite unforeseen, and which is not only very different from, but even quite inconsistent with, the theories (or, in the language of Pareto, the derivations) that they retain continuously throughout the process.

It may be interesting to observe the effect that the evolution of English constitutional history has had on other peoples. In many ways the breach in thought between England and her American colonies took place in the reign of Queen Anne. One can trace it in literature, in religion, and above all in politics; for the doctrine of the separation of the legislative, executive, and judicial powers, as an essential for liberty, remained firmly embedded in the minds of the colonists. That they should not perceive the changes in the parliamentary system, the significance of which the English themselves did not grasp, is certainly not strange, the more so because the three writers already quoted, who were widely read here, insisted on that doctrine and gave no hint of any departure therefrom. Hence when the colonies attained their independence, and set up governments of their own, they based them upon the principles they had inherited from the English revolutionary settlement, which were in fact well suited to the conditions of their life here, and have persisted to the present day.

The effect in Europe was very different. When in the nineteenth century the older forms of monarchical rule were breaking down, and there was a demand for a large popular share in public affairs, men turned their eyes to England and saw a system that seemed to reconcile the forces of progress and order, then much talked of as naturally opposed. It worked smoothly, maintained peace without interfering with liberty, and preserved continuity of administration without blocking change. In short, it appeared to do just what they wanted, and so became a model in the eyes of all men with liberal views. Save, therefore, for Switzerland, which like England had developed an indigenous pattern of her own, it was copied in every European state that introduced popular control of government. But in none of the larger ones, at least, did it produce the fruits of its native soil. For some reason, or for many different reasons, it did not function in the same way, and it proved by no means wholly satisfactory to the people who lived under it, in marked contrast to England, where the system — as a system — has been almost universally esteemed.

The fact is that by a happy accident the parliamentary form of government proved well suited to the temperament of the English people. I call it an accident in the sense that it was not intentionally designed. In any other sense it was not an accident, as the discovery of America by Columbus was not an accident. America was there, the English temperament was there; and if the immediate and very different objects statesmen were striving for had not tended to produce a self-consistent system, one in harmony with the national genius, it would not have evolved as it did. It would in the course of its growth have been diverted into other forms, worse in the long run or better, but different and perchance not self-consistent at all.

In continental Europe, on the other hand, the plan did not grow by constant adaptation to particular needs, but was in general adopted as a model, without a thorough consideration of political conditions or national experience and temperament; and any system so adopted, whether copied or devised, is exposed to an ever present difficulty, because unknown elements always enter into the problem whose importance cannot be ascertained. It is almost impossible to discover in advance what all these elements are and what are their mutual reactions. One is, indeed, liable to find that the factors set down as constants are in fact variables and as such functions of the other variables and of one another. For example, the whole operation of the parliamentary system depends upon the nature, the consistency, and the relations of the political parties. In England there are normally two, those of the government and the opposition, not too far apart to be able to alternate peaceably in power. Out of these the system has grown; it has tended to strengthen them, and is in general accord with the popular tendencies. But in all the larger continental states this has not been so, for there were, and where the system remains there still are, many political groups, some of them irreconcilable. Obviously that presents a very different condition, perhaps one not to be foreseen, but one that changes the nature of the problem.

The object of this paper is not to discuss modern government, but merely to point out that men, like animals, may attain a self-consistent and harmonious system of conducting their affairs by a process of striving for immediate intentional objects, if the conditions happen to be such as to lead to a system of that kind; and this although the actors themselves do not contemplate it, or even if the result is quite contrary to their preconceived ideas.

CULTURE AS A DETERMINANT
OF BEHAVIOR

Bronislaw Malinowski, Ph.D., Sc.D.

Professor of Anthropology, University of London

CULTURE as a determinant of human behavior"—
I read this title as an injunction to prove that there
exists a science of human behavior, which is the science
of culture. Culture, in fact, is nothing but the organized
behavior of man. Man differs from the animals in that he
has to rely on an artificially fashioned environment: on
implements, weapons, dwellings, and man-made means of
transport. To produce and to manage this body of artifacts
and commodities, he requires knowledge and technique.
He depends on the help of his fellow-beings. This means
that he has to live in organized, well-ordered communities.
Of all the animals he alone merits the tripartite title of
homo faber, zoon politikon, homo sapiens.

All this artificial equipment of man, material, spiritual,
and social, we call technically culture. It is a large-scale
molding matrix; a gigantic conditioning apparatus. In
each generation it produces its type of individual. In each
generation it is in turn reshaped by its carriers.

Is this big entity itself subject to laws of a scientific
character? I for one have no hesitation in answering this
question in the affirmative. Culture is a determinant of
human behavior, and culture as a dynamic reality is also
subject to determinism. There exist scientific laws of
culture.

The possibility of a really scientific approach to humanism and anthropology is still contested. It is not super-

fluous, therefore, to reaffirm the existence of determinism in the study of human culture.

In my opinion the principal ailment of all humanism is the disjunction of empirical approach from theory, of methods of observation from speculative doctrine. It will be best, therefore, first to turn to the testimony of cultural fact itself. It is easiest to grasp the essence of a phenomenon in contemplating its manifestations through a wide range of variation. Let us then make a rapid flight over the globe and obtain bird's-eye views of some highly divergent types of human culture.

I. *The Culture of a Nomad Tribe*

Let us descend first on the arid and dusty steppes of central East Africa inhabited by the Masai, the famous fierce warriors of the region. On approaching the native encampment we are met by a group of men, tall, dignified, armed with iron spears and daggers. Their women, svelte and elegant, startle the newcomer with the glitter and rattle of the wrought-iron ornaments encircling their necks, wrists, and ankles. Both sexes still wear the native robes of soft goat- or sheepskin. Not a shred of calico nor European trinket mars the archaic vision of men and women of Africa as they lead us into the ring of low brown huts, made of thatch, plastered with cow-dung, and enclosed with a stout fence of prickly shrub.

Conservative in his material culture, the Masai still clings also to his old tribal ways. He still remains at heart a gentleman robber, herdsman, cattle-lifter, and warrior. When, after years of drought, starvation threatens the Masai among their pestilence-stricken herds, how can they help using force, in which they have been trained through generations, against their fat and flabby neighbors grown weak in their wealth and security? Their whole social organization — age-grades, mutilations and tests of endurance, and military drill — is tuned up to the development of warlike virtues. The Masai warrior — that is, every man between puberty and marriage — lives in a special camp, devoting all his time to the aristocratic arts of doing nothing and preparing for war. He is governed by a democratic regime in which an elected captain administers law and leads the men into battle.

Agriculture they despise, vegetables being food fit only for women. As a Masai warrior put it to me in a convincing argument: "The earth is our Mother. She gives us all the milk we need, and feeds our cattle. It is wrong to cut or scratch her body" — a confirmation of the psychoanalyst's conception of Mother-Earth, by one who had not studied the works of Professor Freud yet!

As to sex morals, they leave entire freedom to immature girls, who consort with the warriors in their camp. At puberty every woman has to undergo a drastic operation, clitoridectomy, which constitutes their marriage rite.

The whole tribe owe allegiance to the *Ol'loibon*, the hereditary rain magician and prophet. He controls them through his gift of divination and his power of producing magical fertility of land and of women.

How can we press this strange, exotic material, as rich and varied and elusive as life itself, into a scientific scheme? The temptation to stop at artistic impressionism is great. We might well feel that it would be best to paint the warlike Masai in exaggerated colors in order to bring out the martial, boisterous, licentious "genius" of this culture.

Indeed, this type of procedure is the latest fashion in anthropology. Since, however, we are in search of a scientific, that is, deterministic approach, let us inquire into what are the main interests of the natives, the pivotal points of their tribal life. We see at once that their interests center around food, sex, defense, and aggression. Divination and prophecy, and their political influence, are related to their military adventures and the vicissitudes of climate. The age-grades are an occupational organization correlated with their military life; they form an educational system in which tribal knowledge is imparted, discipline and endurance inculcated.

Thus culture, as we find it among the Masai, is an apparatus for the satisfaction of the elementary needs of the human organism. But under conditions of culture these needs are satisfied by roundabout methods. The Masai cannot turn to nature directly in order to nourish himself. In the long development of his tribal culture, the institution of pastoralism has come into being. The tending, breeding, exchange, and ownership of cattle, incidentally also the need of its defense and protection, impose derived or secondary imperatives on the life of the Masai: the cattle kraal, military camps, seasonal migrations, and fertility magic are the outcome and correlates of pastoralism.

The continuity of the race equally does not work by physiological determination alone. Sexual appetite and personal attraction, the urge to mate, and the desire for children are reformulated culturally. Each phase of the biological process — maturation, puberty, courtship, marriage, and parenthood — is correlated with the mode of life and the arrangements of domesticity and bachelors' camp; and the whole is safeguarded by the military organization. The vast phenomenon of kinship, including the family, marriage, clanship, and the laws of descent, is the cultural counterpart of the physiological process of reproduction.

II. *The Needs of Man and the Aspects of Culture*

Let us see what the conditions are in a neighboring tribe. Not far from the Masai steppes, on the slopes of the

Kilimanjaro, the highest mountain in Africa, live the Chagga, an agricultural, sedentary people. The Chagga, though he also keeps and appreciates cattle, is mainly a tiller of the soil. Yams and pumpkins, peas and millet thrive well on the fertile green fields of the Kilimanjaro. The staple food, however, is the banana. As the Masai culture has been labeled "cattle-complex," so the Chagga culture could certainly be defined as a banana obsession. The Chagga lives on bananas; he lives among bananas — every homestead must be surrounded by its banana grove; and when he is dead he is buried amid bananas.

In contrast to the nomadic Masai, the Chagga have a highly developed body of land laws. Their large-scale system of irrigation is a feat of engineering unparalleled anywhere in native Africa south of the Sahara. Again, unlike the democratic Masai, the Chagga have a well-developed chieftainship. In each district the chief is the supreme judge, the source of law, the military leader, and the high priest of tribal ancestor-worship. The centralized power of the Chagga, however, is not based on aggressive militarism. They have a highly developed system of defense, with extensive, well-guarded earthworks along the frontiers, and enormous subterranean chambers where men, women, and cattle are able to take refuge during a Masai raid.

The Chagga differ from their neighbors, the Masai: they practice agriculture, live in fixed settlements, have a developed system of land tenure; and their religion consists mainly in ancestor-worship. They resemble the Masai in that they practice female circumcision, they have developed age-grades, and they believe in magic by divination. What is the best way of establishing a common measure for the scientific comparison of differences and also of similarities?

Clearly, again, we must compare their institutions — that

is, the organized systems of activities, each correlated with a fundamental need. In both tribes we find that to nutrition there corresponds the economic system, dominated among the Chagga by agriculture, among the Masai by cattle-breeding. In both cultures we should have to analyze the economic system by means of such universally valid concepts as the organization of production, the methods of distribution, and the manner in which consumption integrates certain groups of people. Among both we should have to consider the physiological process of reproduction as it is organized into the domestic institutions. The physiological growth of the individual is in both cases institutionalized into the system of age-grades. Political organization comes into being in the satisfaction of the need for safety in the case of the Chagga; in the case of the Masai the military organization and the political system are the outcome of a periodic need for predatory economics. In both tribes there are, again, corresponding organizations for the maintenance of internal law and order. The political system, in its military and legal aspects alike, imposes its own discipline, morale, ideals, and economic requirements.

The transmission of the cultural heritage from one generation to another brings into being the two educational systems of the Chagga and Masai. In both tribes the earlier stages of training are bound up with domestic life, while later on the initiations into age-grades carry on the education in tribal custom and morality.

From the comparison of the two cultures we reach one of our pivotal generalizations. Every culture must be analyzed into the following aspects: economics, politics, the mechanism of law and custom, education, magic and religion, recreation, traditional knowledge, technology, and art. And all human cultures can be compared under the headings of this scheme.

Far from the chaotic, indeterministic defeatism which overwhelms the amateur, and apparently even some professional anthropologists, this approach gives us a solid scientific foundation.

Incidentally, we also arrive at another conclusion. Anthropology, the science of culture, must study the same subjects as those which confront the student of contemporary civilization, or of any other period in human history. It must approach primitive culture from the angle of politics and economics, theory of religion, and jurisprudence. And here anthropology may claim a special position among the other sciences of human society and culture.

Its range is the widest; it relies entirely on direct observation, for its sources are in the student's own field. It is perhaps the only social science which can easily remain detached from political bias, nationalist prejudice, sentiment, or doctrinaire zeal. If this social science fails to develop an entirely dispassionate study of its material, there is not much hope for the other branches of humanism. Hence, in vindicating the scientific character of anthropology we are working at the very foundations of social science. Anthropology has the privilege and the duty of acting as an organizing agency in the comparative study of cultures.

III. *Adaptation to Environment and Diseases of Culture*

In order to appreciate the influence of environment upon culture, let us leave tropical Africa and move into the desert of snow, ice, and rock inhabited by the Eskimos. Their winter house, made of stone or of snow, has been described as a marvel of engineering, a perfect adaptation to climate and to the available material. It certainly is an example of thoroughgoing correlation between a material object and the necessities of life. Combining warmth, space, and ventilation, it provides during the long winter night comfortable places in which to lie and listen to the long tales of folklore, or carry on technical activities. The technological excellence of these natives is also shown in the construction of their sledges and their weapons, of their canoes, and of their traps.

In comparison with this, some aspects of their culture seem underdeveloped. The Eskimos have been described as devoid of any political system or of legal institutions. They have been often accused of extreme pacifism in that they do not slaughter each other in organized fighting. Yet this is perhaps not quite correct. For though they have no political chieftainship, they recognize the authority of the Shaman. He also acts in a roundabout way as an important juridical agency. They have their code of law, consisting of many taboos, the breach of which brings down evil not only on the wrongdoer but on the whole community. Tribal calamity can be averted only by public confession. After that the Shaman can magically re-establish tribal prosperity. Thus, as the Masai have anticipated psychoanalysis, so the Eskimos are the forerunners of the Oxford Group movement.

On the other hand, towards sex they have the same attitude as the Masai. They have also a somewhat similar type of political system, always with the exception that the one are extremely warlike, and the others have never heard of fighting.

Our approach to a scientific study of culture, through the various aspects which correspond to the fundamental and derived needs of man, does not break down even here, when we apply it to such a one-sided, in many ways stunted, and in other ways hypertrophied, culture as that of the Eskimos. For the Eskimos eat and reproduce, maintain themselves secure against weather and animals, have

developed means of movement in space, and they also
regulate the bodily development of the individual. Their
culture consists, like all others, of the cardinal aspects:
economics, education, law, politics, magic and religion,
knowledge, crafts, art, and also recreation.

What about war? Some divisions of the Eskimos have
a minimum of military organization. Others are completely ignorant of fighting. Since the polar and central
Eskimos have no neighbors, nor yet any cause for internal
quarrels and dissensions, they cannot have military institutions. This fact confirms our conception of the instrumental nature of organized activities. Where, as in their
westernmost offshoots, the Eskimos are in contact with
warlike Indian tribes, they have developed the organization, the virtues, and the apparatus of war.

In the study of war, as of any other aspect of culture, the
strict application of scientific determinism is necessary.
This is achieved by clear definitions, empirical concepts,
and inductive generalization. All the wrangles as to the
innate pacifism or aggressiveness of primitive man are
based on the use of words without definition. To label all
brawling, squabbling, dealing out of black eye or broken
jaw, *war*, as is frequently done, leads simply to confusion.
One author tells us then that primitive man is a natural
pacifist. Another has recently described war as indispensable for the survival of the fittest. Yet another maintains
that war is the main creative, beneficent, and constructive
factor in the history of mankind. But war can only be defined as the use of organized force between two politically
independent units, in the pursuit of a tribal policy. War
in this sense enters fairly late into the development of
human societies.

Only with the formation of independent political units,
where military force is maintained as a means of tribal

policy, does war contribute through the historical fact of conquest to the building up of cultures and the establishment of states. In my opinion, we have just left this stage of human history behind, and modern warfare has become nothing but an unmitigated disease of civilization.

I have made this brief digression on warfare because it illustrates one side of the scientific or functional method in cultural analysis. This method is often accused of over-emphasizing the perfect integration of all factors within the working whole of culture. This is a misrepresentation. The functional method only insists on the fact that all the elements of culture are related to each other; they are not idle survivals or disconnected traits, but they function — that is, they are at work. It does not pronounce any appreciation or moral comment as to whether this work is good or evil, well or badly adjusted. As in the case of some primitive types of warfare, and certainly of its most recent developments, the instrumental analysis of culture reveals more cogently than dissection into traits the occurrence of catastrophic maladjustments of human society.

As you have noticed just now, and felt, perhaps, throughout the argument of this lecture, there has been a background of critical indictment running right through. I do not want to waste your time with controversy and polemics. At the same time, I do not want you to feel that we are running in open doors in insisting on an objective, sober, empirical, and non-mystical treatment of culture. We are engaged now in laying down the foundations for a sound method in social science. When these are clearly and simply stated, they have a knack of appearing mere truisms. Science in the long run is nothing but common sense and experience built up on a systematic basis, refined and clarified to the utmost limits of conceptual lucidity. So, briefly: I have been insisting that anthropological theory must be objective, which means aboveboard, and presented in a manner amenable to verification. Why? Because some of the leaders of contemporary anthropology still maintain that there is a subjective factor in all humanistic observation. To quote an eminent scholar: "All historical definitions are in their very essence subjective."

I have been driving in the existence of a measure common to all comparative work in anthropology — the existence, that is, of a general scheme of human culture, universally valid. Why? Because it has been stated in so many words that "no common measure of cultural phenomena can be found," and that "the laws of cultural process are vague, insipid and useless."

I have again and again indicated that it is illegitimate to cover our inability to deal with certain facts by such mystic labels as the "genius of culture," or to describe this "genius" as Apollonian, Dionysiac, megalomaniac, or hysterical. Why? Because all these atrocities have been recently committed. Culture has been described as the "collective hysteria" of society. We have had recently a whole rainbow of colorful tags and epithets tied to the neck of each individual culture.

I have insisted that analysis must not be arbitrary; that the dissection of a culture, even as that of a corpse, must obey the laws of its anatomy, and not become mere butchery, a lifting out of "traits" and the lumping of them into haphazard "trait complexes." Why? Because the most powerful school in anthropology still follows the precepts of Graebner, who would have us isolate "traits" and define them by characteristics not founded in the nature of the object or the material. One of the leading American anthropologists tells us that an agglomeration of such traits into a complex "is historically most convincing when the traits are not related to one another." To regard culture as a jumble of disconnected and unrelated details may lead to amusing reconstructions but of doubtful value. In the process, however, it robs our whole concept of culture of all life and significance.

IV. *The Family as the Cornerstone of Social Structure*

But let us leave aside this controversial mood. To make our point clear, let us concentrate on an object — *the* object of objects, in a way — the material embodiment of the premier institution of mankind, the family. We shall choose our example from yet another ethnographic area and contemplate a pile dwelling in Melanesia.

In sharp contrast to the arid steppes of central Africa and the Arctic desert of snow, we are surrounded here by a wilderness of water, coral reef, and swamp. The main symptom of man's adaptation to his surroundings is a remarkable achievement of primitive architecture, the house on piles. It stands firmly on its foundations of stout treetrunks driven deep into the muddy bottom of the lagoon. Constructed of strong material cunningly fitted and lashed together, it resists the combined attacks of wind, waves, and weather.

To the lagoon dweller such a house is a fortress where he can take refuge and which he can defend. It is a watchtower from which he can see the approach of suspicious strangers. It is also conveniently near to the coast which he frequently has to visit in order to tend his gardens. The structure of the house is thus determined by the intertribal relations of the people, their economic pursuits, by climate and natural environment.

It can thus be studied only within its natural setting. But after man has invented, constructed, and improved his dwelling, and made it into a fortress, an economic asset, and a comfortable home, the house then dominates his

whole mode of life. The outer shell of his domesticity influences the social structure of family and kinship.

Indeed, it seems that the higher the cultural development, the more ruthless and brutal becomes the tyranny of
machine over man. Are we not at present hopelessly en-
slaved by our hypertrophied prosperity which we have not
yet learned to manage; by our rapid means of communication which allow us to speed, but too often to speed but
aimlessly? And last, not least, and worst of all, by our ex-
cessive efficiency in the means of collective destruction?
Once more a humanist may be allowed to reflect on the
fact that the overdevelopment of mechanical science and
its applications have completely outgrown the progress of
our knowledge of how to adjust our efficiency to really
human aims and needs.

Since in my opinion anthropology should begin at home,
let me give you an anthropological impression of modern
culture and recount a personal experience in which I very
poignantly became aware of the power of things over man.

No experience in my exotic wanderings among the Tro-
brianders and the Chagga, among the Masai and the
Pueblo, has ever matched the shock I received in my first
contact with American civilization on my first visit to
New York, when I arrived there ten years ago on a fine
spring evening, and saw the city in its strangeness and
exotic beauty. The enormous yet elegant monsters blink-
ing at me through their thousand starry eyes, breathing
white steam, giants which crowded in fantastic clusters
over the smooth waters of the river, stood before me: the
living, dominating realities of this new culture. During my
first few days in New York I could not shake off the feeling
that the strange "genius" of this most modern civilization
had become incarnate in the skyscraper, the subway, and
the ferry boat. Large insects in the shape of automobiles

crept along the gutter called street or avenue, subordinate but important. Finally, as a fairly insignificant and secondary by-product of the enormous mechanical reality, there appeared the microscopic bacteria called Man, sneaking in and out of subway, skyscraper, or automobile, performing some useful service to their masters, but otherwise rather insignificant. Modern civilization is a gigantic hypertrophy of material objects, and contemporary man will still have to fight his battle in order to reassert his dominance over the Thing.

But what interests us at present is to find the existence of a common measure between the residential part of the skyscraper and snowhouse, pile-dwelling and cow-dung hut.

In the material used, in structure, in architecture, in all, that is, which we can call the form of the object, there is hardly one trait in common. But look at the dwelling as a part of an institution. It appears at once that the principles on which each dwelling is integrated into organized human life and becomes the shell of this life are the same throughout humanity. In the penthouse on top of the skyscraper, in the snow igloo, in the *engadji* of cow dung, in the *niyumba* of thatch, we find the same domestic unit, the family, consisting of father, mother, and children.

Is the resemblance only superficial? No. Functionally it is not merely a resemblance, but an identity. The group is united by the same task, the essential business of reproducing the race. A universal type of legal charter gives juridical validity to the group. The act of marriage bestows legitimacy on the children, grants the consorts mutual privileges and duties, defines the domestic work of husband and wife; above all, it imposes on them the duty of looking conjointly after the children. Human parents, unlike animals, are not allowed merely to throw up fresh organisms, but they have to introduce fully fledged citizens into the community.

Another fundamental difference between man and the animals is that under civilization parenthood develops into the wider network of relations which we anthropologists call the system of kinship. Here at once a universal generalization can be made. In every human society both parents share in procreation, in tending and training the children, but only one line of descent is legally relevant. Kinship is counted either in the direct mother line or father line. And the anthropologist is also able to state the reason why. Any ambiguity, any confusion in the tracing of filiation inevitably leads to disaster and chaos in laws of inheritance and of succession. Even as it is, with one line of descent, primogeniture, or with the law of borough-English, ultimogeniture, most legal difficulties in primitive and developed communities are due to conflicts in the law of inheritance or succession.

Another universal law of kinship is that, under unilateral descent and the classificatory system of kinship status, parenthood becomes extended into clan relationship. The classificatory use of kinship terms, again, a curious linguistic phenomenon which seems to saddle every individual in primitive culture with a whole bunch of fathers and mothers, of aunts, uncles, sisters, and, alas, even mothers-in-law, is universal. To explain it whole libraries have been written about the existence of primitive promiscuity, group marriage, and the gradual development of monogamy out of complete sexual and parental communism. All this is, in plain American, *bunkum*! Had the classificatory system been discovered by one who spoke the native language well, had it been studied scientifically, a very simple explanation would have been discovered.

The discovery of the actual live function of classificatory

themselves to other things, fishing and trapping, industries, canoe-building, and trading expeditions. One man only, the Garden Magician, still remains hard at work. He has been in fact from the beginning an organizer of work, directing the allotment of land, and, while ostensibly he was carrying on his rites, in reality he acted as tribal entrepreneur. Even when it comes to the harvest he still has to bless the crops and then perform over the stored produce a type of magic which, by reducing the appetite of the people, makes food last longer.

But agriculture as an economic activity does not end with the harvest. The distribution of the products is an important business which penetrates into all the aspects of tribal life. Tribute has to be given to the chief, and on this tribute his political power is largely based. A quota of food has to be put aside for tribal ceremonies, and this finances largely their public and religious activities. Finally, the third stage of the economic process, consumption, presents many interesting aspects in this tribe, as everywhere else. For consumption means not merely eating, but also handling, display, ritual food offerings, and last but not least, sheer waste. For in the Trobriands the passion for accumulated food is so great that people prefer to keep their yams till they rot in the storehouses rather than to see the latter empty.

We see, then, that agriculture must be studied within the context of the whole economic system. For the vegetables are exchanged for fish; they are used in the financing of enterprise and for feeding the craftsmen, for the capitalization of industries. This is especially interesting in the study of the large native jewelry, or, more correctly, tokens of wealth, which play a considerable part in the political system and which are also ceremonially exchanged in the course of large inter-tribal expeditions, which are practiced throughout this region. Could we apply the same detailed study to Masai or to Chagga economics, or those of the Eskimos or Plains Indians, we would see that they also must be considered under the three headings of production, distribution, and consumption.

In production we would find everywhere the question of the social and cultural forces by which labor is organized. We would have to inquire how productive labor is maintained; in other words, whether there are beginnings of capital and even of interest. Under the heading of distribution, we would not merely have to consider the complicated institutions of African marketing, peddling, and hawking, as well as more or less extensive forms of intertribal trade. We would also have to discuss the chief's tribute.

I think that throughout the world we would find that the relations between economics and politics are of the same type. The chief, everywhere, acts as a tribal banker, collecting food, storing it, and protecting it, and then using it for the benefit of the whole community. His functions are the prototype of the public finance system and the organization of state treasuries of today. Deprive the chief of his privileges and financial benefits, and who suffers most but the whole tribe? At the same time, it would be interesting to see how sometimes, especially in African monarchies, the chief's political power was abused for selfish and extortionate financial policy; and equally interesting to see what limits there were to such malpractices. In the few cases where I was able to investigate into this matter in central East Africa, I found that the subjects could, and did, rebel, or else used sorcery, of which the monarch was usually very much afraid.

As regards consumption, we should find that the common eating of food, its preparation and the joint domestic

that
con
wo

without any claims to the fruits of their labor. But such communism turns men into slaves, serfs, or pawns. May this not be true of all forms of communism?

Another interesting lesson which we can learn from an anthropological survey is in the analysis of profit. We are often told that with the abolition of private profit all evils, such as war, sexual jealousy, poverty, and even drunkenness, will disappear. There is no doubt at all that profit lends itself to abuse through dishonest financial manipulation and the running, in the interest of shareholders, of enterprises which ought to be directed to public service. It must be controlled by public agencies in primitive as well as in civilized communities. But is it necessary to change the whole social order, nationalize all wealth and means of production, in order to reach the desired end? To me the Marxian doctrine of profit entails a complete misconception of the relationship between the economic factor and other motives and drives in human society. The pocket is not the only channel by which wealth can be maldistributed and abuses canalized. Vanity, doctrinaire zeal, incompetence, and personal ambition cause as much havoc as does greed. The men who control production — in Africa or Europe, in Melanesia or America — do not and cannot fill their pockets or bellies with gold. Where they can and do harm is in mishandling and misusing the production and distribution of wealth. In order to prevent that, public control by disinterested agencies is necessary. And here it is obviously better to have a system in which control of wealth, legislation, and the executive use of power are not concentrated in the same hands, but vested in separate agencies. The totalitarian state and the African autocracy are not models of sound economic systems. The real advance lies in the gradual piecemeal reform, involving all the parts of the economic and political organism. An integral revolution destroys, but it does not create. The concentration of all controls in the same hands means the abolition of all control.

VI. *Savage Exoticisms and Scientific Anthropology*

So far we have concentrated on prosaic, ordinary, non-savage aspects. Many of you who have come to see a notorious anthropologist perform on the platform have, no doubt, drawn up a hopeful list of anticipations: cannibalism, couvade, avoidance of the mother-in-law, and the pious custom of killing and eating aged and decrepit parents, head-hunting and infanticide, sorcery, trial by ordeal, human sacrifice, taboos, totems, and all the other tricks of trade of the entertaining anthropologist. It all started with Herodotus, who amused us with talks about lotus-eaters and man-eaters, about queer sexual habits and gastronomic perversions.

I have been drab and sober on purpose. If anthropology is to become the comparative science of cultures, it is high time it stepped out of its herodotage and anecdotage. It must turn to the fundamentals of human culture, in simple and complex, primitive and highly developed forms alike. It must study primitive economics and political systems, the theory of kinship and social organization, early jurisprudence, and systems of education. It must study all of these across the widest comparative range of human experience.

Not that we could not profitably dwell on some of the primitive eccentricities of man. Cannibalism as a system of foreign policy is a sound way of solving international complications: it is a rapid and effective manner of assimilating racial and national minorities. To run away from or to turn your back on your mother-in-law, many of us feel, would be an amiable and highly rational way of securing

What was the effect of his imprecations on the wind does not matter to us skeptics, but the effect of his voice on the human beings was truly magical. His voice rose like a mighty wall of safety between the frightened human beings and the unchained forces of nature. It was evident that the villagers now felt safe. They became more and more calm and reassured as the magician proceeded with his long spell. They behaved quite differently after the magic had been chanted. And immediately after he had finished his spell the magician took the practical situation in hand: he gave orders what to do, orders which were immediately obeyed in a disciplined, organized manner.

I realized then and there what the real function of magic is. On the psychological side it leads to a mental integration, to that optimism and confidence in the face of danger which has won to man many a battle with nature or with his human foes. Socially, magic, by giving leadership to one man, establishes organization at a time when organized and effective action is of supreme importance.

We have seen exactly the same function of magic in Trobriand agriculture. There also the magician acts as organizer to the community, while to each individual he gives confidence, spurring him to greater effort. And here I would immediately like to add a rider. If we were to examine either the wind magic or the agricultural magic point by point, we should come to one extremely important conclusion. The activity of the magician never encroaches on the technique or subject matter of practical work. In agriculture the Trobriand magician bestows additional fertility on the soil, forestalls pests and blights, the ravages of bush pigs and wallabies, destruction by drought and other unmanageable causes. He never does magic instead of cutting down the shrub or fertilizing the soil with ashes.

Magic is always carried out on the principle "Magic

helps those who help themselves." It deals with the un-accountable, unmanageable elements of luck, chance, and misfortune. It never tackles the ordinary forces of nature, which are always managed by man with his own hands. Exactly the same may be said of the magic of war, of love, of enterprise, and of health. Everywhere magic only steps in where knowledge has declared its inability to deal with the situation. Far from being an assertion of the omnipotence of thought, it is rather a humble declaration that man throws himself on the mercies of higher super-natural forces, revealed through sacred tradition.

We define magic as the ritual act performed to bring about a practical result unachievable by man's unaided force. The ritual act is based on the belief that by the strict observance of traditionally prescribed behavior, bodily and verbal, man can influence the course of nature and the rulings of fate. This belief is always founded on traditional mythology and on the empirical affirmation of the power of magic. Magic has its ethical value in that it affirms the positive issues and thus leads to courage, en-durance, and perseverance. It also makes people join in ritual work for the common good.

To define religion quite briefly, it differs from magic in that it does not aim at practical ends in emergencies of ordinary life. Religion, indeed, deals with the permanent and enduring problems of human existence. The acts of religion are not means to a practical end. Each religious ritual is an end in itself; in communion with divinity, in sacrifice the worshipper ministers to the pleasure of his god or gods; in acts of ancestor-worship homage is made and union achieved with the spirits of the dead. Each of such acts brings about its own end and compensation. In one important branch of religious activities, those connected with the death of a human being, we also see that mourn-

we bound, and what is the sense of all man's fears, suffer-
ings, and disappointments?   Metaphysics and religious
speculation are as old as knowledge and as old as language
itself.   At the beginning they are extremely simple and
crude. Animism and beliefs in magical force, fantasies about
sorcery, ghosts, vampires, and totemism — that is, the belief in the spiritual affinity between man and nature — are
the answers of primitive man to the fundamental riddles of
life. Once we realize their real nature it is easy to perceive
their great value.   They are well adapted to the limited
conditions in which primitives have to live, they contain
the answer to the questions of whence and whither, and
above all they supply man with ritual means of getting in
touch with spiritual forces, of establishing communion with
ancestral spirits, totemic beings, or divinities, and they
allow man to secure his immortality and thus to give sense
to his life.

Knowledge, magic, and religion are the highest, the most
derived imperatives of human culture.   Indirectly and
through several relays they also are the outcome of man's
organic needs.   The craving for religion and for magical
power, and scientific curiosity as well, are not instinctive.
They are the outcome and the correlate of that intelligent
adjustment of man to his environment which makes him
the master thereof.   Magic and to a much higher degree
religion are the indispensable moral forces in every human
culture. Grown out, as they are, of the necessity to remove
internal conflict in the individual and to organize the community, they become the essential factors of spiritual and
social integration. They deal with problems which affect
all members of the community alike. They lead to actions
on which depends the welfare of one and all. Religion and
to a lesser extent magic thus become the very foundations
of culture.

IX. *Summary and Conclusions*

By now, I trust, we all realize that there exist laws of cultural process, and that their discovery is the main task of scientific anthropology.

I have started with the affirmation that there is a science of culture. I hope that throughout the succeeding pictures of living cultures with their variety and diversity of forms, throughout the analysis of what these cultures have in common and how they differ, we have all realized that there is an underlying fundamental sameness; that it is possible to establish the common measure which is indispensable for the scientific treatment of any type of reality.

We have found everywhere that observation can be made fruitful, relevant, and convincing only if it is inspired by a theory of the nature of culture. Culture in the first place has to satisfy the organic needs of man. From the indirect, that is cultural, satisfaction of these, there arise further instrumental imperatives. Finally, in the spiritual realm, culture implies the integrative principles of knowledge, religion, ethics, and magical technique. Every human culture can be analyzed by the same universally valid concepts, derived from a theory which again consists of a system of general laws. At the same time, we have found that there is only one type of really scientific theory, and that is a theory which is dictated by observation and which can be tested by it.

The general concepts and laws I need not summarize for you. They result from the universal occurrence of such aspects of human culture as economics and education, law and political organization, magic, religion, art, and recreation. The cultural activities, again, in every society integrate into natural units, which we have called institutions. And here again it is possible to draw up a list or table of

such institutions. The family, the extended kinship grouping, the clan, the village community, the tribe, and the
nation are such universal institutions. If we add to them
such more diversified types as occupational groups, economic teams, voluntary associations, we have a number of
cultural entities each of which is amenable to laws and
generalizations, and each of which must be studied by the
same outfit of concepts.

In the vast system of institutional activities which corresponds to the fact of reproduction, we have listed such
laws as the dominance of the initial situation; the principle of legitimacy, defining the legal aspect of parenthood;
the further principle that marriage leads to the establishment of a domestic unit; the concept of the unilateral and
bilateral kinship principles in reproduction, and the principle that the clan is not equivalent in influence to the
family, but a derivate.

Whether we study economics as an aspect or whether we
proceed to the definition of such specific economic institutions as agriculture, cattle-breeding, the organized activity of the hunting team, we can and must base our studies
on a series of general laws or principles. We have to inquire into the economic process in its three phases: production, distribution and exchange, and consumption. We
have to study these three phases as they permeate the
whole of tribal life. We cannot understand the titles to
property except through the role which they play in production and the influence which production exercises on
property. Again, we find that unless we consider economics
in conjunction with the organizing forces of religion and of
magic, of law and politics, we shall always miss some of the
most important realities of economics.

Had we more time, we should have been able to construct equally exhaustive theories of primitive law and

primitive education, of the part played by recreation in primitive societies, and of the principles of artistic activities in their social and cultural aspect.[1]

In the course of our analysis we have had to emphasize the point that every cultural phenomenon presents to us three main facts: the material, the social, and the spiritual. The first is best approached through the analysis of the material substratum of culture; the second by the study of institutions; the third through the linguistic approach. For, although I am not a behaviorist, I believe that it is best to study mental processes in their objective, outward manifestations.

Thus I maintain that the subject-matter of the comparative study of cultures does lend itself to sober, scientific treatment. I also maintain that this treatment is indispensable, especially from the point of view of actual research in the field.

I have tried to define the scope of anthropology, the pioneer among social sciences in the empirical approach to determinism. Determinism does exist in cultural process, and the scientific statement of this process must be deterministic, objective, fully documented, and unaffected by personal and impressionistic distortion. Scientific anthropology, as you have seen, must work on the foundations laid down by biology and physiology; it must work hand in hand with the psychologist; and it must learn as much as it can learn from the student of environment, the geographer.

Our plea for scientific anthropology, of course, is not tantamount to an indictment or exorcism of all the attrac-

[1] The reader might perhaps compare my *Crime and Custom in Primitive Society* (1926); the article, "Kinship," in *Man* (1930), p. 19, where a bibliography of my publications on kinship will be found; and the small book, "The Definition of Culture," shortly to be published.

tive and amusing speculations. Evolutionary *aperçus*, indeed, I regard as indispensable. Careful and sober diffusionist hypotheses seem to me quite profitable. To minimize or discard a really human interest in humanism would be a crime. To mix up or confuse the emotional or artistic approach with the scientific is a serious lack of judgment. The two approaches must be used simultaneously; they have to complement each other. But science must furnish the foundation.

The scientific theory of culture has also brought to light some really vital truths. Is the recognition of the universal stability and permanence of the family and marriage of no interest in these days when domestic institutions seem to be threatened on every side? The anthropologist might almost add: "As it was in the beginning, is now and ever shall be." That communism cannot be a panacea for all our cultural troubles may also be an interesting appreciation. We have seen that communism alone is never to be found in any culture, however primitive or complex. We have seen, also, why communism as an economic system cannot work except in conjunction with slavery. On the other hand, pure individualism does not exist anywhere either. So that some admixture of communism, that is, public control, has always worked and worked well. But it cannot work wonders, or cure all evils. We have defined the role of the supernatural as an integrating and organizing force in society. One of the implications of our analysis was that the abuse of law and political power must always lead to cultural disaster. Science and virtue, efficiency and endurance, courage and chastity can never be dictated by edicts, nor enflamed by oratory, nor yet forced into existence by a system of police spies and police brutalities. To replace religion and morality by the secret service of a totalitarian state is a disease of culture.

For we have fully acknowledged the existence of cultural maladjustment, and even of lethal ailments of civilization. The very concepts of adaptation and function imply degrees and qualifications, from excellence to decay.

Our present civilization is undoubtedly passing through a very severe, perhaps a critical stage of maladjustment. The abuse of legal and administrative power; the inability to create lasting conditions of peace; the recrudescence of aggressive militarism and magical trickery; the torpor of true religion and the assumption of a religious garb by doctrines of racial or national superiority, or the gospel of Marx — all this shows that, while we have become the masters of inanimate nature, we have connived at the complete enslavement of man by machine.

The greatest need of today is to establish a balance between the stupendous power of natural science and its applications, and the self-inflicted backwardness of social science and the consequent impotence of social engineering. To repeat a truism just mentioned, we have allowed the machine to overpower man. One of the reasons for this is that we have learned to understand, hence to respect and to handle, the mechanism. But we have failed to develop the really scientific spirit in humanism.

Today the freedom to exercise purely scientific determinism is threatened in many countries. This freedom is even more essential for social than for natural science. It is, therefore, our duty on this occasion to insist on the necessity for this freedom. We are assembled here to celebrate the tercentenary of one of the greatest workshops of science and reason ever established by man. The founding of Harvard was an act of human behavior not outside reason and determinism. It was determined by wise foresight, and its existence and work have been enduring factors in developing reason and determining rational behavior. Harvard has always fostered that spirit of science which means freedom in the search for truth, for the laws of nature and of human behavior. Let this spirit preside over the development of the comparative science of man, and we may yet hope that the spirit of Harvard — that is, the spirit of science—will prevail in the conduct of human affairs.

PERSPECTIVES IN SOCIAL INQUIRY

CLASSICS, STAPLES AND PRECURSORS IN SOCIOLOGY

Authority and the Individual.   1937

Baldwin, James Mark.   **The Individual and Society:** Or,Psychology and Sociology.   1911

Beaglehole, Ernest.   **Property:** A Study in Social Psychology.   1932

Beard, Charles A.   **The Nature of the Social Sciences:** In Relation to Objectives of Instruction.   1934

Burrow, Trigant.   **The Biology of Human Conflict:** An Anatomy of Behavior, Individual and Social.   1937

Carr-Saunders, A. M.   **The Population Problem:** A Study in Human Evolution.   1922

Carver, Thomas Nixon.   **The Essential Factors of Social Evolution.** 1935

Congress of Arts and Science: Selected Papers.   1906

De Man, Henry.   **The Psychology of Socialism.**   [1928]

Factors Determining Human Behavior.   1937

Giddings, Franklin Henry.   **The Scientific Study of Human Society.** 1924

Hayward, F[rank] H.   **Professionalism and Originality.**   1917

Huntington, Ellsworth.   **World-Power and Evolution.**   1920

Hurry, Jamieson B.   **Poverty and Its Vicious Circles.**   1917

Jenks, Edward. **The State and The Nation.** 1919

Judd, Charles Hubbard. **The Psychology of Social Institutions.** 1927

Kelsen, Hans. **Society and Nature:** A Sociological Inquiry. 1946

Lange, Frederick Albert. **The History of Materialism:** And Criticism of Its Present Importance. 3 vols. in 1. 1879-1881

Le Bon, Gustave. **The Psychology of Peoples.** 1924

Lewis, George Cornewall. **An Essay on the Influence of Authority in Matters of Opinion.** 1849

Lewis, George Cornewall. **A Treatise on the Methods of Observation and Reasoning in Politics.** 2 vols. in 1. 1852

Lowell, Abbot Lawrence. **Public Opinion in War and Peace.** 1923

Maine, Henry Sumner. **Village-Communities in the East and West.** 1889

Merton, Robert K. and Paul F. Lazarsfeld, eds. **Continuities in Social Research:** Studies in the Scope and Method of "The American Soldier." 1950

Michels, Roberto. **First Lectures in Political Sociology.** 1949

Ogburn, William Fielding and Alexander Goldenweiser, eds. **The Social Sciences and Their Interrelations.** 1927

Park, Robert Ezra. **The Collected Papers of Robert Ezra Park.** 3 vols. in 1. 1950/52/55

Plint, Thomas. **Crime in England:** Its Relation, Character and Extent as Developed from 1801 to 1848. 1851

Ranulf, Svend. **The Jealousy of the Gods and Criminal Law at Athens.** 2 vols. in 1. 1933/34

Ross, Edward Alsworth. **Social Psychology:** An Outline and Source Book. 1912

Small, Albion W. **General Sociology.** 1905

Studies in Social Psychology in World War II: Vols. I, II, and III. 1949

Sutherland, Alexander. **The Origin and Growth of the Moral Instinct.** 2 vols. in 1. 1898

Tarde, G[abriel]. **Social Laws:** An Outline of Sociology. 1899

Teggart, Frederick J. **Prolegomena to History.** 1916

Thomas, William I. **Sex and Society.** 1907

Von Wiese, Leopold. **Systematic Sociology.** 1932

Ward, Lester F. **Applied Sociology.** 1906

Wirth, Louis, ed. **Eleven Twenty-Six:** A Decade of Social Science Research. 1940

Wright, R[obert] J[oseph]. **Principia, Or Basis of Social Science.** 1875